# Finance in Continuous Time

## *A Primer*

$$df(X) = f_x(X)\,dX + (1/2)f_{xx}(X)\,dX^2$$

## David C. Shimko

# Finance in Continuous Time
## *A Primer*

# Finance in Continuous Time
## *A Primer*

David C. Shimko

University of Southern California

 Kolb Publishing Company

Library of Congress Catalog Card Number 91-75348.

Printed in the United States of America.


ISBN: 1-878975-07-2

 Kolb Publishing Company
7175 S.W. 47th St., Suite 210   Miami, Florida  33155
KOLB   (305) 663-0550    FAX (305) 663-6579

*To my wife, Deborah*

*and to the memory of*

*Daniel Siegel,*

*my mentor and friend*

# Preface

This text is intended for Ph.D. students in finance and other students of continuous-time methods with an interest in finance. The theory of continuous-time methods is presented only to the extent that the practitioner can improve intuition and apply the valuation and problem-solving methods to interesting problems in finance. Technical points are explored more thoroughly in advanced texts; the reader is encouraged to study these texts listed in the bibliography. This primer contains many examples and exercises for the beginning practitioner, complete with worked solutions and citations to the finance literature.

Continuous-time methods provide a powerful analytical tool for the description and solution of financial problems. These methods have been applied to the valuation of derivative securities, the valuation of cash flows, the equilibrium description of markets, optimal investment strategies, optimal financing strategies, and many other issues.

A number of brilliant textbooks have been written to teach students of finance (broadly defined) how to use these methods; one of these textbooks should be used as a primary basis of study in a continuous-time course. This primer attempts to make the continuous-time intuition and calculus more accessible to students in these courses of study. The primer has a "do-it-yourself" orientation that prods the student to value financial assets himself, and not merely shrug his shoulders after he derives the differential equation for the asset value. The viewpoint of this text is quite applied; theory is presented only to the extent that theory can facilitate thoughtful and rigorous application. The text concentrates particularly on the valuation of cash flows as a basis for all financial asset valuation problems.

An ideal background for the text is the following:

1. A basic knowledge of financial valuation techniques
2. Familiarity with discrete-time stochastic processes
3. Facility with calculus
4. Exposure to partial differential equations

The fourth item is slightly less important for this text; if the student is willing to apply himself to the solution of a few of these equations, he will find ample help within this text.

Who should read this book? First, Ph.D. students in finance. Secondly, finance faculty in other subspecialties who want to gain some familiarity with continuous-time methods in finance. Thirdly, technical finance professionals with an interest in financial asset valuation. Fourthly, mathematicians or physicists with an interest in applying continuous-time methods to financial problems.

For the sake of expositional convenience, the pronouns "his," "himself," and "he" are used to refer to any individual of either sex. Masculine genes are not prerequisites for the study of continuous-time finance!

For maximum benefit, all problems in the text should be solved; complete solutions can be found at the end of each chapter. I have taught the course in this book in five weeks in my Ph.D. class at the University of Southern California, and I followed the book with several papers from the bibliography. Both students and finance faculty attended. Their encouragement and contributions led to the publication of this text.

Companion study and further study may make use of one of the following texts:

Dothan, Michael U., *Prices in Financial Markets*, Oxford University Press: New York, 1990.

Huang, Chi-fu and Robert H. Litzenberger, *Foundations for Financial Economics*, North Holland: New York, 1988.

Ingersoll, Jonathan E., Jr., *Theory of Financial Decision Making*, Rowman and Littlefield: Totowa, NJ, 1987.

Merton, Robert C., *Continuous-Time Finance*, Basil Blackwell: Cambridge, MA, 1990.

# Acknowledgments

Special thanks go to students in the University of Southern California Ph.D. class who helped develop and field-test the problems in the text: Lynn Laber, Rameshwar Singh, Mei-Wen Wang, and Charles Woodhouse. I thank the faculty members who encouraged me to convert the class notes into a text. I thank Larry Harris, who proofread earlier versions of the text. Peter Carr (Cornell University), Francis Longstaff (Ohio State University), and Robert McDonald (Northwestern University) field-tested the text. I thank them and their students for their comments.

The following people served as reviewers for the text. Their detailed comments were invaluable in improving the flow and precision of the text. Of course, remaining errors are entirely my responsibility.

| | |
|---|---|
| John Marshall | St. John's University |
| Ricardo Rodriguez | University of Miami |
| Eduardo Schwartz | University of California at Los Angeles |
| Daniel Siegel | University of Washington |

I also thank Robert Kolb, the publisher, for seeing value in this text and making a commitment to realize that value. Kateri Davis typeset the manuscript and was instrumental in completing the project. Andrea Coens edited the successive drafts to ensure continuity. To both Kateri and Andrea, my deepest appreciation for helping bring the book to life. Personal thanks (as always) extend to my ever-encouraging wife Deborah, and my newest sources of inspiration, Arielle Sara and her new twin brothers, Eitan Benjamin and Zev Naftali.

David C. Shimko
University of Southern California

# Contents

# 1

# A Paradigm for Primary Asset Valuation

## Introduction

We begin with the assumption that the reader either is familiar with stochastic processes in discrete time or has experience in time series analysis. We use the discrete-time processes to motivate intuition for the continuous-time processes; the reader then discovers how these processes might be applied to variables of financial interest. The properties of arithmetic Brownian motion (random walk), geometric Brownian motion (proportional random walk), and the Ornstein–Uhlenbeck processes (mean–reverting) are presented so that the reader may check the formulation of financial models for economic meaningfulness.

An elementary form of the famous Itô's Lemma is presented in Section 3, along with its multivariate extensions and extension to jump processes. This section motivates the intuition behind Itô's Lemma and facilitates student understanding. The chapter ends with financial applications of Itô's Lemma and by showing how to derive some elementary asset prices.

The chapter should be read in its entirety, since later sections depend critically upon developments in earlier sections. Students should attempt all problems at the end of the chapter.

# Discrete and Continuous Models

We begin by considering the discrete–time random walk description:

$$W(t + 1) = W(t) + e(t + 1); \quad W(0) = W_0 \quad e \sim \text{i.i.d. } N(0,1)$$

The variable t represents time and is measured in discrete integer
increments from $-\infty$ to $\infty$. For convenience, we take time 0 as the
present. The random variable $e(t)$ is serially chosen from a normal
(Gaussian) distribution with mean zero and unit variance. The
draws through time are independent of each other and identically
distributed (i.i.d.).

$W(t)$ is the level of the cumulant of $e(t)$;[1] it is called a
**random walk** because it appears that W takes random steps up and
down through time, as if wandering aimlessly. The process can be
used to describe many variables. Physicists use the random walk to
describe the univariate position of a particle. Early stock market
theorists used the random walk to describe the level of stock
prices: If changes in price are unpredictable, then stock price levels
follow a random walk. Figure 1.1 shows an example of a random
walk simulated in discrete–time increments (with zero mean and
unit variance). We have not yet specified the unit of time; clearly,
if t increases at monthly increments, a refinement of the data might
be desirable for smaller time increments. We explore this possibility by allowing = 1/n for an arbitrary integer n > 1. We would like
to describe a process that has the same characteristics as the
random walk but observed more frequently:

$$W(t + \Delta) = W(t) + e(t + \Delta); \quad W(0) = W_0, \quad e \sim \text{i.i.d. } N(0,\Delta)$$

This newly defined process has the same expected drift and
variance over n periods as the first process has over one period.

---

[1]Assuming $W(0) = W_0 = 0$

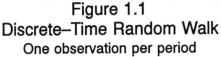

## Figure 1.1
## Discrete–Time Random Walk
### One observation per period

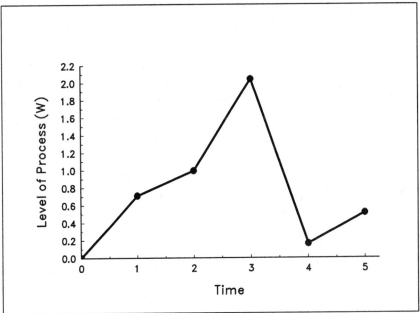

To illustrate our point, we examine a process that is the same as that in Figure 1.1 but observed four times as frequently. In other words, every fourth observation from Figure 1.2 is shown in Figure 1.1. In the econometrics literature, such a process is called an *aliasing* process.

Now consider the behavior of the process as $\Delta \to dt$:

$$W(t + dt) = W(t) + e(t + dt);$$
$$W(0) = W_0, \quad e \sim \text{i.i.d. } N(0,dt)$$

and define $dW(t) \equiv W(t + dt) - W(t)$. We heuristically define dt as the smallest positive real number such that $dt^\alpha = 0$ whenever $\alpha > 1$. Either of these processes, $dW(t)$ or $e(t + dt)$, is referred to as *white noise*. Obviously, the graph of the process as $\Delta \to dt$ cannot be shown. However, a high-frequency aliasing process can be shown in Figure 1.3 that resembles the continuous process more closely.

## Figure 1.2
## Discrete–Time Random Walk
### Four observations per period

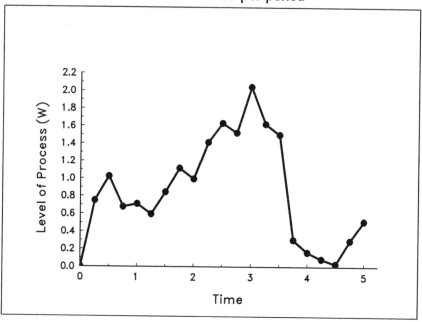

Recall that dW may be thought of as a normally distributed random variable with mean zero and variance dt. We note six properties that follow by construction:

1.  $E[dW(t)] = 0$
2.  $E[dW(t)dt] = E[dW(t)]dt = 0$
3.  $E[dW(t)^2] = dt$

Property 1 follows by construction; the mean of this normally distributed variable is zero. Property 2 uses the property that the expectation of the product of a random variable (dW) and a constant (dt) equals the constant times the expected value of the random variable. Property 3 uses the property for any distribution with zero mean that the expected value of the squared random variable is the same as the variance.

## Figure 1.3
## Discrete–Time Random Walk
### Approaching Continuous Limit

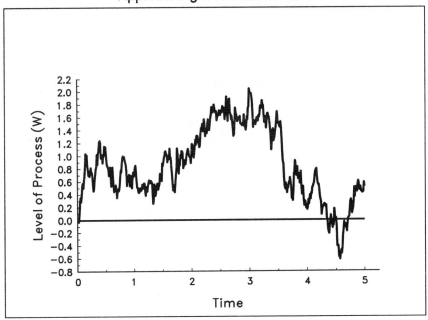

4. $\text{Var}[dW(t)^2] = E[dW(t)^4] - E^2[dW(t)^2] = 3\,dt^2 - dt^2 = 0$

5. $E[(dW(t)dt)^2] = E[dW(t)^2]\,dt^2 = 0$

6. $\text{Var}[dW(t)dt] = E[(dW(t)dt)^2] - E^2[dW(t)dt] = 0$

Property 4 follows from the knowledge of the fourth central moment of the standard normal distribution ($\mu_4 = 3$), and the heuristic definition of dt that provides that $dt^2 = 0$. Property 5 follows immediately from Properties 2 and 3. Property 6 follows from Properties 2 and 5.

These properties are important because they demonstrate that the variance of a function of a random variable vanishes in Properties 4 and 6. Also, the expectation operator is redundant if the variance of a random variable is zero. Therefore, we have

$$E[f(dW)] = f(dW) \text{ if } \text{Var}[f(dW)] = 0$$

These properties give rise to three multiplication rules:

Rule 1.  $dW(t)^2 = dt$

Rule 2.  $dW(t)dt = 0$

Rule 3.  $dt^2 = 0$

The first two multiplication rules simply eliminate the redundant expectation operator from Properties 2 and 3. Properties 4 and 6 allowed us to eliminate the expectation operator, because they show that the variance of these random variables vanishes. The third multiplication rule follows our heuristic definition of dt.

The process W(t) is referred to as a *standard Wiener process*. It can be represented either in differential form:

$W(0) = W_0$; dW(t) is a standard Wiener process

or integral form:

$$W(t) = W_0 + \int_0^t dW(u)$$

In this primer, differential notation will be used, although the integral representation is more precisely defined in the stochastic processes literature.

The standard Wiener process has many properties, some of which are provided below. Be sure to confirm your intuition with Figure 1.3.

1.  W(t) is continuous in t.
2.  W(t) is nowhere differentiable.
3.  W(t) is a process of unbounded variation.
4.  W(t) is a process of bounded quadratic variation.
5.  The conditional distribution of W(u) given W(t), for u > t, is normal with mean W(t) and variance (u - t).

6.   The variance of a forecast W(u) increases indefinitely as
     $u \rightarrow \infty$.

Property 1 holds because dW, although it is a random variable,
is of infinitesimal magnitude. W is not differentiable (Property 2)
since the left and right differentials are not the same; they are
independent random variables. Property 3 states (without proof in
this text) that the continuous random walk path has infinite length.
However, Property 4 states that the sum of squared changes in W
is finite, and does in fact equal t.

Properties 5 and 6 discuss the distribution of W(u) given W(t)
for u > t. Recall that W is an integral (i.e., a sum) of random
variables dW. The sum of normally distributed random variables is
also normal: the mean of the sum is the sum of the means, and the
variance of the sum equals the sum of the variances if the correlations are all zero. This is the same as Property 5. Property 6 simply
mentions the property that the variance of an ever–expanding sum
of normally distributed independent random variables will grow
indefinitely.

The standard Wiener process is inappropriate for much
financial modeling. However, we can write quite general continuous stochastic processes as functions of standard Wiener processes.
For example, consider once again a discrete random walk with
generalized drift and heteroscedasticity (i.e., changing variance) that
depend on both X(t) and t:

$$X(t + 1) = X(t) + \alpha(X(t),t) + \sigma(X(t),t) \, e(t + 1);$$
$$X(0) = X_0, \; e \sim \text{i.i.d. } N(0,1)$$

If we choose a subinterval of length $\Delta$ that mimics the behavior of
this process, we can write:

$$X(t + \Delta) = X(t) + \alpha(X(t),t)\Delta + \sigma(X(t),t) \, e(t + \Delta);$$
$$X(0) = X_0, \; e \sim \text{i.i.d. } N(0,\Delta)$$

By **mimicking** we mean that the stochastic properties of periodic samples from a more frequently observed process would be the same as those observed in the less frequently observed process, provided the observation interval were the same. Strictly speaking, the mimicking is only accurate if $\alpha$ and $\sigma$ are constants; the purpose here is to build intuition for the development of stochastic models. As we let $\Delta \rightarrow dt$, we see that:

$$dX(t) = \alpha(X(t),t)\ dt + \sigma(X(t),t)\ dW(t);\ X(0) = X_0$$

which is the description of a generalized univariate Wiener process. From this point forward, we will drop 't' as an argument of the X and W processes; the time dependence will be understood:

$$dX = \alpha(X,t)\ dt + \sigma(X,t)\ dW;\ X(0) = X_0$$

Throughout this text, we will use dW and dZ as standard Wiener processes. dX and dY refer to functions of the standard processes.

How can we interpret the statement "$dX = \alpha\ dt + \sigma\ dW$"? Suppose for the moment that $\alpha$ and $\sigma$ are constant. The term dW is a normally distributed random variable, with mean zero and variance dt. The statement says that dX is also a random variable, a linear function of a normal random variable, which is itself normally distributed. The random variable dX has mean "$\alpha\ dt$" and variance "$\sigma^2\ dt$".

In ordinary statistical parlance, the statement that "$X = \mu + z\sigma$" represents a standard expression of a normally distributed variable as a function of a standard normal random variable "z". The variable z has mean zero and unit variance, but X has mean $\mu$ and variance $\sigma^2$. At an intuitive level, the statements "$X = \mu + z\sigma$" and "$dX = \alpha\ dt + \sigma\ dW$" are perfectly analogous.

The difficulty lies in changing levels of $\alpha$ and $\sigma$; changes may depend on the level of X, the passage of time, or both. The accumulation of these normal random variables can yield distributions of future values that follow many distributions. The next section discusses the most frequently occurring accumulations.

# Frequently Occurring Continuous Stochastic Processes

### Arithmetic Brownian Motion $\qquad$ dX = α dt + σ dW

Let $\alpha(X,t) = \alpha$ and $\sigma(X,t) = \sigma$, two constants. Then the process X is said to follow arithmetic Brownian Motion with drift $\alpha$ and volatility $\sigma$. The process is an appropriate specification for economic variables that grow at a linear rate and exhibit increasing uncertainty. The process X has the following properties (among others):

1. X may be positive or negative.
2. If u > t, then $X_u$ is a future value of the process relative to time t. The distribution of $X_u$ given $X_t$ is normal with mean $X_t + \alpha(u - t)$ and standard deviation $\sigma\sqrt{(u - t)}$.
3. The variance of a forecast $X_u$ tends to infinity as u does (given t, $X_t$).

The three properties indicate that arithmetic Brownian motion is appropriate for variables that can become positive or negative, have normally distributed forecast errors, and have forecast variance that increases linearly in time. For example, net cash flow might be appropriately modelled as following arithmetic Brownian motion, but revenues would not be appropriate.

Figure 1.4 demonstrates a sample arithmetic Brownian motion path with positive drift ($\alpha > 0$).

### Geometric Brownian Motion $\qquad$ dX = αX dt + σX dW

Let $\alpha(X,t) = \alpha X$ and $\sigma(X,t) = \sigma X$. The process X is then said to follow geometric Brownian motion with drift $\alpha$ and volatility $\sigma$. The process is appropriate for economic variables that grow exponentially at an average rate of $\alpha$ and have volatility proportional to the level of the variable. The process also exhibits increasing forecast uncertainty.

## Figure 1.4
### Arithmetic Brownian Motion
Drift = 0.296; Volatility = 10%

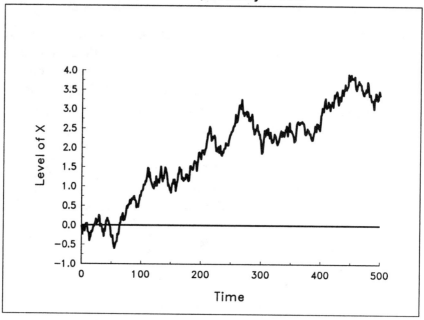

The process X has the following properties (among others):

1. If X starts at a positive value, it will remain positive.

2. X has an absorbing barrier at 0: Thus, if X hits 0 (a zero-probability event), then X will remain at zero.

3. The conditional distribution of $X_u$ given $X_t$ is lognormal. The conditional mean of $\ln(X_u)$ for $u > t$ is $\ln(X_t) + \alpha(u - t) - \frac{1}{2}\sigma^2(u - t)$ and the conditional standard deviation of $\ln(X_u)$ is $\sigma\sqrt{[u - t]}$. $\ln(X_u)$ is normally distributed. The conditional expected value of $X_u$ is $X_t\exp[\alpha(u - t)]$.

4. The variance of a forecast of $X_u$ tends to infinity as u does.

Geometric Brownian motion (GBM) is often used to model security values, since the proportional changes in security price are

### Figure 1.5
### Geometric Brownian Motion
Drift = 0.296; Volatility = 10%

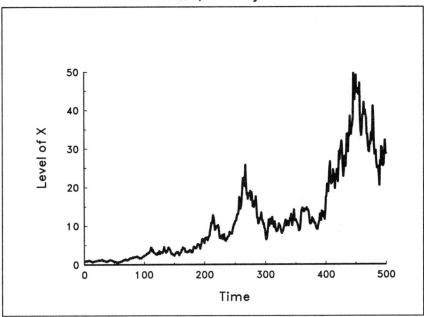

independent and identically normally distributed. It can also be used to model anything that is positive and increases (on average) at a constant exponential rate. For example, one could use GBM to model the nominal price of a commodity or the revenue from a particular activity. Also, for some cases, a negative growth rate is desired for a positive variable; GBM may be appropriate here as well. In Figure 1.5, we use the same random numbers as Figure 1.4 does to demonstrate what an equivalent geometric Brownian motion might look like.

## Mean Reverting Process    $dX = \kappa(\mu - X) \, dt + \sigma X^{\gamma} \, dW$

The mean reverting process is also called the Ornstein-Uhlenbeck process when $\gamma = 1$. Let $\alpha(X,t) = \kappa(\mu - X)$ and $\sigma(X,t) = \sigma X^{\gamma}$, where $\kappa \geq 0$ and $\gamma$ is arbitrary. The process $X$ is then said to follow a a mean-reverting process with speed-of-adjustment parameter κ, long run mean μ, and volatility σ. The choice of γ may lend further interpretation to the volatility of the process. This process is an appropriate specification for positive economic variables that tend toward a long-run mean value but may be beset by short-term disturbances. We assume that κ, μ, and γ are positive. The process exhibits the following properties (among others):

1. X is positive as long as X starts positive.

2. As X approaches 0, the drift is positive and volatility vanishes.

3. As u becomes infinite, the variance of a forecast $X_u$ is finite.

4. If $\gamma = \frac{1}{2}$, the distribution of $X_u$ given $X_t$ for $u > t$ is non-central $\chi^2$; the mean of the distribution is:

$$(X_t - \mu)\exp[-\kappa(u - t)] + \mu,$$

and the variance of the distribution is:

$$X_t(\sigma^2/\kappa)(\exp[-\kappa(u - t)] - \exp[-2\kappa(u - t)]) + \mu(\sigma^2/(2\kappa))(1 - \exp[-\kappa(u - t)])^2.$$

(See Cox, Ingersoll, and Ross 1985b for complete descriptions.)

The mean-reverting process is appropriate for interest rates or inflation rates, for example, that may have stable long-run values and do not represent traded assets. We could also model volatility itself (if volatility changes unpredictably) as a mean-reverting process. Using the same random numbers as in Figures 1.4 and 1.5, we can show what a mean-reverting square root process might look like in Figure 1.6.

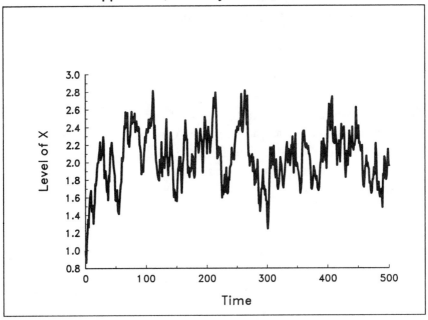

Figure 1.6
Mean–Reverting Square Root Process
Kappa = 0.1; Volatility = 10%; Mean = 2

## Itô's Lemma and Its Multivariate Extensions

We consider a real-valued function $f(X):\mathbf{R}\to\mathbf{R}$, where X is a generalized Wiener process. Using Taylor's Series expansions to estimate $f(X + \Delta)$, we see:

$$f(X + \Delta) = f(X) + \Delta f_x(X) + \tfrac{1}{2}\Delta^2 f_{xx}(X) + \tfrac{1}{2}\,\Delta^3 f_{xxx}(X) + \ldots$$

where subscripts denote derivatives (later partial derivatives). Standard calculus allows $\Delta\to dX$ and provides that $dX^2$ [i.e., $(dX)^2$] and higher powers vanish, therefore:

$$f(X + dX) = f(X) + f_x(X)\,dX \quad or \quad df(X) = f_x(X)\,dX$$

However, in stochastic calculus, the term $dX^2$ does not vanish, even though higher order terms still vanish. Intuitively, dX is small enough in ordinary calculus such that $(dX)^2$ is sufficiently close to zero. In stochastic calculus, dX is a normally distributed random variable. Since the variance is positive, $(dX)^2$ does not disappear, but converges in probability to dt.

The fundamental theorem of *stochastic* calculus states that:

$$f(X + dX) = f(X) + f_x(X)\,dX + \tfrac{1}{2}f_{xx}(X)\,dX^2 \;\; or,$$
$$df(X) = f_x(X)\,dX + \tfrac{1}{2}f_{xx}(X)\,dX^2$$

This is a logical extension of the Fundamental Theorem of Calculus. It is known as the simplest form of Itô's Lemma.

If a variable t were deterministic, then the term $dt^2$ would vanish; we can use this property to extend Itô's Lemma to functions of X and t:

$$f = f(X,t)$$
$$df = f_x dX + f_t dt + \tfrac{1}{2}[f_{xx}dX^2 + 2f_{xt}dXdt + f_{tt}dt^2]$$

Because $dXdt = 0$ and $dt^2 = 0$, the expression simplifies further:

$$df = f_x dX + f_t dt + \tfrac{1}{2}f_{xx}dX^2$$

We write $dX = \alpha\,dt + \sigma\,dW$, where $\alpha$ and $\sigma$ are functions of X and t. Then, using the multiplication rules on page 6, we have:

$$dX^2 = (\alpha dt + \sigma dW)(\alpha dt + \sigma dW) =$$
$$(\alpha dt)^2 + 2\alpha\sigma dtdW + (\sigma dW)^2 = \sigma^2 dt$$

Therefore, df can be written:

$$df = [\alpha f_x + \tfrac{1}{2}\sigma^2 f_{xx} + f_t]\,dt + \sigma f_x\,dW$$

This is also called the law of motion for f(X), and is an alternate form of Itô's Lemma. Intuitively, df shows the change in value of a function of X through time, where X follows a generalized Wiener process. Since f may depend explicitly on time, part of the changes to f derive from the passage of time. However, the passage of time affects the level of X and, therefore, affects f indirectly as well. Itô's Lemma represents a summary of the relevant effects on changes in the value of f.

If we introduce a second stochastic variable Y to the system that follows a generalized Wiener process, we have:

$$dX = \alpha(X,Y,t) \, dt + \sigma(X,Y,t) \, dW$$
$$dY = \beta(X,Y,t) \, dt + v(X,Y,t) \, dZ$$

where dZ is also a standard Wiener process. We define $dZdW = \rho dt$ as the correlation between the two processes. This construction is quite reasonable. Recall that the expected value of the product of two random variables is equal to the correlation if their means are zero and their variances are one. It is easy to show that $E[(dZdW)^2] = 0$, so that $E[dZdW] = dZdW = \rho dt$.

Probabilistically, dZ can be expressed as a function of its projection onto dW plus an independent residual:[2]

$$dZ = \rho \, dW + \sqrt{(1 - \rho^2)} \, de$$

where de is a standard Wiener process independent of dW ($dedW = 0$).[3] The multivariate extension to a function $f(X,Y,t)$ has the following Itô differential:

$$f = f(x,y,t)$$
$$df = f_x dX + f_y dY + f_t \, dt + \tfrac{1}{2}[f_{xx} dX^2 + 2f_{xy} dXdY + f_{yy} dY^2]$$

---

[2]To prove this construction is valid, calculate its mean, variance, and correlation with dW. All the moments are the same on the left and right sides of the equation.

[3]Recall that for jointly distributed normal random variables that zero covariance implies independence.

Terms of order higher than $\alpha = 1$ for $dt^\alpha$ vanished, as before. Using our multiplication rules we have a recap:

| Multiplication | dW | dZ | dt |
|:---:|:---:|:---:|:---:|
| dW | dt | $\rho$ dt | 0 |
| dZ | $\rho$ dt | dt | 0 |
| dt | 0 | 0 | 0 |

Therefore:

$$dX^2 = (\alpha dt + \sigma dW)^2 = \sigma^2 dt, \quad dY^2 = (\beta dt + v dZ)^2 = v^2 dt$$

and:

$$dXdY = (\alpha dt + \sigma dW)(\beta dt + v dZ) = \sigma v \rho \, dt$$

Making all the appropriate substitutions, we have:

$$df = [\alpha f_x + \beta f_y + f_t + \tfrac{1}{2}\sigma^2 f_{xx} + \rho \sigma v f_{xy} + \tfrac{1}{2}v^2 f_{yy}] \, dt$$
$$+ \sigma f_x \, dW + v f_y \, dZ$$

The last equation is a multivariate extension of Itô's Lemma. However, it is often easier to remember the Taylor–series–like expansions shown above. For an arbitrary stochastic variable $Z$, terms of order higher than $dZ^2$ vanish, while if $Z$ is deterministic, terms of order higher than $dZ$ vanish.

## An Introduction to Jump Processes

While the previous generalized Wiener process includes a broad family of possible continuous processes, it is occasionally of interest to study processes that change discretely at infrequent intervals. The Poisson process is ideally suited to this kind of study. We define $q$ so that $q$ starts at 0 and increases by steps of

1 every time a Poisson event occurs. In its simplest form, a Poisson process with a constant intensity parameter $\lambda$ provides that:

$$dq(t) = 1 \text{ with probability } \lambda dt$$
$$= 0 \text{ with probability } 1 - \lambda dt$$

at every moment in time, where $dq(t)$ is the instantaneous change in q in moment t. For now, we take $\lambda$ as constant. As usual, we drop the functional dependence of q on t from the notation. Figure 1.7 presents a sample realization of a standard Poisson process which jumps by unit values at randomly determined exponential inter-arrival times.

We now introduce a random variable with compact support called $\xi(X,t)$. A random variable has compact support if the domain over which the random variable has positive probability measure

### Figure 1.7
### Sample Standard Poisson Process
Unit increments; $\lambda = 0.5$

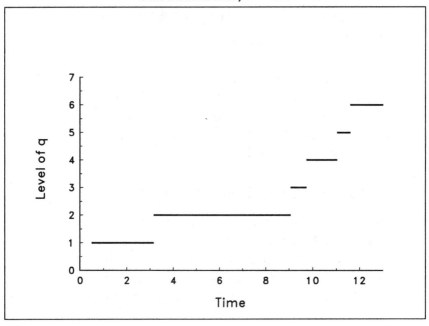

is a compact set. A compact set is one that is closed and bounded. We can write a process X that contains both continuous and discontinuous changes as:

$$dX = \alpha dt + \sigma dW + \xi dq$$

implying that X jumps by an amount $\xi$ whenever a Poisson event occurs. For example, in default, a security may jump in value to zero. If X is the value of the security, then $\xi = 0 - X$, or $-X$. We can interpret the statement to mean that dX is equivalent to the sum of a normally distributed random variable with mean $\alpha dt$, variance $\sigma^2 dt$, and an occasional shock (probability $\lambda\,dt$) of level $\xi$.

For real-valued functions $f(X)$, the change in function value conditional on the occurrence of an event is $f(X + \xi) - f(X)$; therefore, the expected change in function value is:

$$\lambda dt E[f(X + \xi) - f(X)] + (1 - \lambda dt)[0] = \lambda E[f(X + \xi) - f(X)]dt$$

The expected squared change in function value does not vanish; we cannot, therefore, claim that the expectation is redundant. In financial modelling, we often assume this residual risk is diversifiable. That is, no investor cares about this risk in the pricing of securities. We also need to assume that the timing of the jump and the level of X are independent of each other. However, we may allow $\lambda$ to depend on X or follow its own stochastic process.

With this in mind, the appropriate version of Itô's Lemma can be stated:

$$f = f(X,t,q)$$
$$df = f_x dX + \tfrac{1}{2}f_{xx}dX^2 + f_t dt + [f(X + \xi) - f(X)]dq$$

We calculate the expected functional change for our purposes, and express df the reduced form:

$$df = \{f_x\alpha + \tfrac{1}{2}f_{xx}\sigma^2 + f_t + \lambda E[f(X + \xi) - f(X)]\}\ dt + f_x\sigma dW$$

# Simple Financial Applications of Itô's Lemma

## Example A

We begin with a deterministic example. Suppose that a security with value V guarantees $1dt every instant of time forever. This is the continuous-time equivalent of a risk-free perpetuity of $1. If the risk-free interest rate is a constant r, what is the (discounted) value of the security?

## Solution

1.  Write the law of motion for V

    $V = V(t)$    (*because V does not depend on any stochastic variable*)

    $dV = V_t dt$    (*subscripts of V denote partial derivatives*)

2.  Calculate E[dV], the expected capital gain on V

    $$ECG = E[dV] = V_t dt$$

3.  Calculate the expected cash flows to V

    $$ECF = 1\ dt$$

4.  Calculate the total return on V

    $$TR = ECG + ECF = [V_t + 1]\ dt$$

5.  Set the total return equal to the risk-free dollar return on V, or rV dt

    $$rV\ dt = [V_t + 1]\ dt$$

6.  Divide both sides by dt; this gives us a differential equation whose value V must satisfy. Solve the differential equation for V. (*Use guessing method, Laplace Transform method, and/or*

*composition of homogeneous and specific solutions. See Chapter 2.)*

$$rV = V_t + 1$$

Guess that V does not depend on time, so $V_t = 0$; then $V = 1/r$, the present value of a risk-free perpetuity in discrete time.

## Example B

Suppose X follows geometric Brownian motion with drift $\alpha$ and volatility $\sigma$. A security with value V collects Xdt continuously forever. V represents a perpetuity that grows at an average exponential rate of $\alpha$, but whose risks in cash flow variations are considered diversificable. The economy is risk-neutral, and the risk-free interest rate is constant at r. What is the value of this security?

We follow the same steps diagrammed earlier:

1.  $V = V(X)$

    *(Because V is a perpetual claim, its value may not depend on time; therefore V is a function of X and not of t.)*

    $$dV = V_x dX + \tfrac{1}{2}V_{xx}dX^2$$
    $$dX = \alpha X dt + \sigma X dW; \; dX^2 = \sigma^2 X^2 dt$$
    $$dV = [\alpha X V_x + \tfrac{1}{2}\sigma^2 X^2 V_{xx}]dt + \sigma X V_x dW$$

2.  $ECG = E[dV] = [\alpha X V_x + \tfrac{1}{2}\sigma^2 X^2 V_{xx}]dt$ *(since E(dW)=0)*

3.  $ECF = X \, dt$ *(by construction)*

4.  $TR = ECG + ECF = [\alpha X V_x + \tfrac{1}{2}\sigma^2 X^2 V_{xx} + X]dt$

5.  $rVdt = [\alpha X V_x + \tfrac{1}{2}\sigma^2 X^2 V_{xx} + X]dt$

6.  $rV = \alpha X V_x + \tfrac{1}{2}\sigma^2 X^2 V_{xx} + X$

Guess that doubling X will double V. If V is proportional to X, then $V = \gamma X$, $V_x = \gamma$, and $V_{xx} = 0$.

Substituting, we get $r\gamma X = \alpha\gamma X + X$ or $\gamma = 1/(r - \alpha)$.

Therefore, $V = X/(r - \alpha)$, the present value of a perpetuity growing at exponential rate $\alpha$ and discounted to the present at rate r.

## Example C

Modify example B to provide for a sudden possible drop to zero in the value of V. If a Poisson event occurs, one gives up V in exchange for nothing. The gain is zero and the loss is V, so the change in the value of V is 0 - V or -V. The possibility of this jump in any instant is $\lambda dt$. Following the steps above, we have:

1.  $V = V(X,q)$  *(not t because of the perpetual nature of V)*

    $$dV = V_x dX + \tfrac{1}{2}V_{xx}dX^2 + [0 - V]\, dq$$
    $$dV = [\alpha X V_x + \tfrac{1}{2}\sigma^2 X^2 V_{xx} - \lambda V]dt + \sigma X V_x dW$$
    *(taking the q expectation)*

2.  $ECG = E[dV] = [\alpha X V_x + \tfrac{1}{2}\sigma^2 X^2 V_{xx} - \lambda V]dt$

3.  $ECF = X\, dt$

4.  $TR = ECG + ECF = [\alpha X V_x + \tfrac{1}{2}\sigma^2 X^2 V_{xx} - \lambda V + X]dt$

5.  $rVdt = [\alpha X V_x + \tfrac{1}{2}\sigma^2 X^2 V_{xx} - \lambda V + X]dt$

6.  $(r + \lambda)V = \alpha X V_x + \tfrac{1}{2}\sigma^2 X^2 V_{xx} + X$

This is the same equation as example B, but with $(r + \lambda)$ taking the place of r.

Therefore, $V = X/(r + \lambda - \alpha)$. We discount the cash flows at a higher discount rate $(r + \lambda)$ to compensate for the possibility of full default. Alternatively, we adjust the growth rate to $(\alpha - \lambda)$ and discount at the risk-free rate. In the second interpretation, $(\alpha - \lambda)$ is the *certainty–equivalent* growth rate.

**Example D**
Suppose X follows geometric Brownian motion, and an independent Poisson process determines the timing of cash payments equal to the contemporaneous value of X. Let V represent the claim to the first cash flow in this stochastic perpetuity. What is the value of V? Following the same steps, we have:

1.  $V = V(X,q)$ *(not t because of the perpetual nature of V)*

    $$dV = V_x dX + \tfrac{1}{2}V_{xx}dX^2 + \lambda[X - V]dt$$

    *(Note: We give up the asset (V) to receive the payment (X).)*

    $$dV = [\alpha X V_x + \tfrac{1}{2}\sigma^2 X^2 V_{xx} + \lambda X - \lambda V]\, dt + \sigma X V_x\, dW$$

2.  $ECG = E[dV] = [\alpha X V_x + \tfrac{1}{2}\sigma^2 X^2 V_{xx} + \lambda X - \lambda V]\, dt$

3.  $ECF = 0$ *(no continuous cash payments)*

4.  $TR = ECG + ECF = [\alpha X V_x + \tfrac{1}{2}\sigma^2 X^2 V_{xx} + \lambda X - \lambda V]\, dt$

5.  $rV\, dt = [\alpha X V_x + \tfrac{1}{2}\sigma^2 X^2 V_{xx} + \lambda X - \lambda V]\, dt$

6.  $(r + \lambda)V = \alpha X V_x + \tfrac{1}{2}\sigma^2 X^2 V_{xx} + \lambda X$

This is the same as Example B, except for two substitutions:

a.  $(r + \lambda)$ takes the place of r
b.  The value of V is multiplied by $\lambda$ (the "cash flow" term is $\lambda X$ instead of X)

Therefore, $V = \lambda X/[r + \lambda - \alpha]$. Check by substituting back into the differential equation: $V_X = V/X$, and $V_{XX} = 0$. If we define $\gamma = (r - \alpha)/\lambda$, we have $V = X/(1 + \gamma)$. This can be compared to the discrete time result; a single payment of X in one period has a value of $X/(1 + r)$ if the payment is risk-free.

Normally, the partial differential equations are more difficult to solve; Chapter 2 discusses the most commonly occurring ones. Also, we failed to specify boundary conditions in these examples, and often, small changes in boundary conditions have great impact on final valuations.

What have we done in this chapter? We studied present value calculations in continuous–time settings. All the securities were perpetual in some sense, although we also discussed potentially perpetual securities with random expiration times. The perpetual nature of these securities yielded ordinary differential equations (ODEs) to solve for asset values. These ODEs can be solved by many methods, but clever guesswork is best.

The paradigm is most important: in a risk–neutral economy, calculate the expected capital gain on an asset from Itô's lemma, add the expected cash flows to get total return, and set total return equal to the risk-free return. This process determines the appropriate ODE to solve for asset value.

## Exercises

1.1 Assume X follows geometric Brownian motion, with drift $\alpha$ and volatility $\sigma$. Let $Y = \ln(X)$, the natural log of X.
   a.  What process does Y follow?
   b.  What is the distribution of $Y_u$, given $Y_t$ and $t < u$?
   c.  What is the expected value of $X_u$, given $X_t$ and $t < u$? (*HINT: If z is distributed $N(\mu, \sigma^2)$, then it must be the case that $E[e^z] = \exp[\mu + \frac{1}{2}\sigma^2]$.*)

1.2 Assume that X follows arithmetic Brownian motion with drift $\alpha$ and volatility $\sigma$. A security V pays Xdt forever. If X becomes negative, the holder of the asset must make payments to the security issuer. The economy is risk-neutral, and the risk-free discount rate is r.
   a.  What is the value of V? (*HINT: V is linear in X; follow example B.*)

b.  Suppose the security holder has the right to abandon the
    asset if cash flows become sufficiently negative, i.e., when
    $X = q$ ($q < 0$). What is the value of V?

    *(HINT: $V = k_1 exp[k_2(X - q)] + k_3 X + k_4$. Note that $k_2 <
    0$. Also, when $X = q$, $V(X) = 0$. Check that the ODE is
    satisfied.)*

c.  If q can be chosen optimally, what is the value-maximiz-
    ing choice? Verify the second order conditions.

d.  What is the value of the abandonment option? *(HINT:
    Look at your answers to parts a and b.)*

1.3 Assume that X follows geometric Brownian motion, with drift
    $\alpha$ and volatility $\sigma$. The economy is risk-neutral, and the
    risk-free rate of interest is r. A machine prints a certificate
    worth X(t) at random times t generated by a Poisson arrival
    process with intensity $\lambda$.

a.  What is the value of the machine? *(HINT: By how much
    should the asset value change at the time the certificate is
    printed?)*

b.  What is the value of a contingent claim to the first
    certificate printed by the machine?

c.  Assume Y follows geometric Brownian motion with drift
    $\beta$ and volatility v. The correlation between X and Y is 0.
    What is the value of a certificate produced by X, if it lets
    its bearer (only) have X certificates printed by machine Y
    (worth Y at the time of printing)? Y prints at the same
    average rate, and the number of certificates is determined
    by the first arrival time.

1.4 A low-risk health insurance policyholder realizes medical
    losses at random times according to a Poisson arrival process.
    The level of the loss is given by X, a process which follows
    geometric Brownian motion with drift $\alpha$ and volatility $\sigma$. The
    economy is risk-neutral, and the risk-free discount rate is r.
    Medical expenses occur at a rate of $\lambda dt$. There is an additional

possibility that the claimant will suddenly become a high risk claimant. High risk claimants experience the same possible losses X, but at a higher frequency, $\mu dt$. The timing of the switch from a low-risk policyholder to a high-risk policyholder is governed by a Poisson process with intensity parameter $\eta$.

a.  If the policyholder stays low-risk all his (infinite) life, what is the value of the policy today?

b.  What is the value of a high-risk policy today?

c.  What is the value of a policy to a low-risk individual who may later become a high-risk individual? (*HINT: The value is a linear function of X.*)

1.5  Assume that the value of an index X follows geometric Brownian motion with drift $\alpha$ and volatility $\sigma$. An asset V promises that, when X reaches Q, the bearer will be paid R and the asset will be retired. The economy is risk-neutral, and the risk-free discount rate is r.

a.  What is the value of the asset? (*HINT: $V = AX^\gamma$, where A and $\gamma$ are positive constants. Also, the boundary condition requires $V(Q) = R$.*)

b.  What are sufficient conditions for $\gamma > 0$?

1.6  Assume that the value of an index X follows geometric Brownian motion with drift $\alpha$ and volatility $\sigma$. A perpetual call option is written such that when it is exercised (at X = Q), the holder of the option receives Q - E, a positive amount. E is the exercise price of the option. The economy is risk-neutral, and the risk-free rate is r.

a.  What is the value of the option, assuming it is exercised when X = Q? (*HINT: Let $V = AX^\gamma$, where A and $\gamma > 1$ are positive constants. Also, V(X) satisfies the boundary condition that $V(Q) = Q - E$.*)

b. Assuming the holder of the call option will act to maximize the current value of his option, what Q will he choose? *(HINT: Use ordinary calculus techniques.)*

c. What are sufficient conditions for $\gamma > 1$?

d. Verify that the value satisfies the ODE you derived.

e. What are the comparative static properties of the model?

1.7 Assume X follows geometric Brownian motion, with drift $\alpha$ and volatility $\sigma$. Assume Y follows geometric Brownian motion with drift $\beta$ and volatility v. The correlation between the Wiener components of the two processes is $\rho$; $dZ_x dZ_y = \rho dt$.

a. Write down the laws of motion for the system.

b. Let V = XY. What process does V follow? Define your process (i.e., define $\alpha_v$, $\sigma_v$, and $dZ_v$) so that it can be written as $dV/V = \alpha_v dt + \sigma_v dZ_v$.

c. What are the correlations of dV with dX and dY?

d. Let W = X/Y. What process does W follow? Organize your results as in part b.

e. What are the correlations of dW with dX and dY?

f. Run a theoretical regression of dY/Y on dX/X. What are your coefficients? What is the standard error of the regression? What are the time series properties of the volatility of the projection (i.e., the error term)? What is the theoretical $R^2$?

1.8 *(Difficult; complete problem 1.3 before beginning.)*
A security with value V pays ydt continuously until x reaches the point q. y follows arithmetic Brownian motion with drift $\alpha$ and volatility $\sigma$, and x follows arithmetic Brownian motion with drift $\beta$ and volatility w. The correlation between the two processes is $\rho$.

a. What ODE must V satisfy?

  b. What are the boundary conditions?

  c. Value the asset.

1.9 *(Difficult; complete problem 1.2 before beginning.)*
  A firm enjoys earnings of Xdt continuously, where X follows arithmetic Brownian motion with drift $\alpha$ and volatility $\sigma$. This is the only asset of the firm. If X becomes negative, then the firm must decide whether to honor its obligations or abandon its operations. We assume it is optimal to abandon operations when earnings fall below a constant level q.

  The firm wishes to sell contingent claims against its earnings. To value an arbitrary contingent claim, we first value four primitive contingent claims with the following cash flows:

$$g_1(X) = 1$$
$$g_2(X) = X$$
$$g_3(X) = I_{\{X>c\}}$$
$$g_4(X) = X\,I_{\{X>c\}}$$

$I_{\{A\}}$ is an indicator function equal to one on set $\{A\}$ and zero otherwise. $g_1$ receives \$1dt until X = q, when it receives nothing. $g_2$ receives X until X = q; if X < 0, the cash is paid instead of received. $g_3$ receives \$1dt if X is above a fixed level c, and is worthless when X reaches q. $g_4$ receives \$Xdt as long as X exceeds a fixed level c, and is worthless when X reaches q.

  Let $Y_i(X)$ represent the value of a claim giving rise to cash flows of $g_i(X)$. We explicitly allow for the optimal abandonment of cash flows; $Y_i$ must satisfy the boundary condition $Y_i(q) = 0$ when X reaches the abandonment point q. We also require $Y_{iX} < \infty\ \forall X > q$. Note: $Y_{iX} \equiv \partial Y_i/\partial X$.

a. What is the value of each of the $Y_i(X)$? Let $\delta = r - \alpha$.
   (*HINT 1: The form of each solution is:*

   $$V = A_1 exp(k_1 X) + A_2 exp(k_2 X) + A_3 X + A_4$$

   *Assume a different form of the solution holds when $X > c$ and when $X < c$.*)
   (*HINT 2: The solution should be continuous and continuously differentiable at $X = c$*)

b. The contingent claimholders are equityholders, debtholders (who have been promised cdt forever), the government, and third parties. The marginal tax rate is $\theta$. The distribution of earnings occurs instantaneously and is as follows:

| Case | Debt | Equity | Government | Third |
|------|------|--------|------------|-------|
| $c < X$ | c | $(1 - \theta)(X - c)$ | $\theta(X - c)$ | 0 |
| $q < X < c$ | $X - k$ | 0 | 0 | k |

   Using the primitive securities in part A, value each of the claims against the earnings of the firm.

c. (Optional) Find the operating and capital structure policy (i.e., levels of q and c) that maximizes the sum of debt and equity values. Write down the first order conditions for an interior maximum only.

## Solutions to Exercises

1.1 a. (Use Itô's Lemma) $dX = \alpha X dt + \sigma X dZ$;

   $dY = (\alpha - \tfrac{1}{2}\sigma^2)dt + \sigma dZ$

b. Normal, mean $Y_t + (\alpha - \tfrac{1}{2}\sigma^2)(u - t)$, variance $\sigma^2(u - t)$.

c. $E[e^y] = exp[Y_t + \alpha(u - t)] = X_t exp[\alpha(u - t)]$

1.2 a. $rV = \alpha V_x + \tfrac{1}{2}\sigma^2 V_{xx} + X$; let $V = AX + B$; $V = X/r + \alpha/r^2$

   b. $k_1 = -q/r - \alpha/r^2$

      $k_2 = [-\alpha - \sqrt{(\alpha^2 + 2r\sigma^2)}]/\sigma^2$

      $k_3 = 1/r$

      $k_4 = \alpha/r^2$

   c. $q^* = 1/k_2 - \alpha/r$

   d. $k_1 \exp[k_2(X - q^*)]$; $k_1 = -1/(rk_2)$

1.3 a. $V = \lambda X/(r - \alpha)$

   b. $V = \lambda X/(r + \lambda - \alpha)$

   c. $V = \lambda^2 YX/[(r + \lambda - \beta)(r + \lambda - \alpha)]$

1.4 a. $\lambda X/(r - \alpha)$

   b. $\mu X/(r - \alpha)$

   c. $rV = \alpha X V_x + \tfrac{1}{2}\sigma^2 X^2 V_{xx} + \eta[\mu X/(r - \alpha) - V] + \lambda X$;

      $V = X[\eta\mu/(r - \alpha) + \lambda]/[r + \eta - \alpha]$

1.5 a. $\tfrac{1}{2}\sigma^2 X^2 V_{xx} + \alpha X V_x - rV = 0$;

      $\gamma = \{(\tfrac{1}{2}\sigma^2 - \alpha) + \sqrt{[(\alpha - \tfrac{1}{2}\sigma^2)^2 + 2r\sigma^2]}\}/\sigma^2$

      $V = R(X/Q)^\gamma$

   b. Sufficient conditions are $\sigma > 0$ and $r > 0$.

1.6 a. $V = (Q - E)(X/Q)^\gamma$, $\gamma$ as defined in 1.6

   b. $Q^* = E\gamma/(\gamma - 1)$

   c. Sufficient: $\sigma > 0$ and $r > \alpha$

   e. $V$ increases in $X$, decreases in $E$, increases in $r$ and $\sigma$.

1.7 a. $dX = \alpha X dt + \sigma X dZ_x$; $dY = \beta Y dt + vY dZ_y$;

      $dZ_x dZ_y = \rho dt$.

   b. $dV/V = \alpha_v dt + \sigma_v dZ_v$; $\alpha_v = \alpha + \beta + \sigma v\rho$; $\sigma_v^2 = \sigma^2 + v^2 +$
      $2\rho\sigma v$

$dZ_v = (\sigma dZ_x + v dZ_y)/\sigma_v$; Check that $E[dZ_v] = 0$, $E[dZ_v^2]$
$= 1$, $E[dZ_v dZ_x] = (\sigma + v\rho)/\sigma_v$, and $E[dZ_v dZ_y] = (v + \sigma\rho)/\sigma$

c.   $dVdX = VX\sigma(\sigma + \rho v)dt$; $dVdY = VYv(v + \rho\sigma)dt$

d.   $dW/W = \alpha_w dt + \sigma_w dZ_w$; $\alpha_w = \alpha - \beta - \sigma v\rho + v^2$;
$\sigma_w^2 = \sigma^2 + v^2 - 2\sigma v\rho$

e.   $dWdX = \sigma XW(\sigma - v\rho)dt$; $dWdY = vWY(\sigma\rho - v)dt$

f.   $dY/Y = \beta dt + v dZ_y$; $dX/X = \alpha dt + \sigma dZ_x$;
$dZ_y = \rho dZ_x + \sqrt{(1 - \rho^2)}dZ_e$; $dZ_e dZ_x = 0$
constant $= [\beta - \alpha v\rho/\sigma]$, slope $= v\rho/\sigma$,
standard deviation of residual $= v\sqrt{(1 - \rho^2)}$
$R^2 = \rho^2$. (*HINT: $R^2$ = explained variation/total variation. The residuals are identically normally distributed and serially uncorrelated.*)

1.8 a.   $V_x\beta + \frac{1}{2}V_{xx}w^2 + V_y\alpha + \frac{1}{2}V_{yy}\sigma^2 + V_{xy}\rho\sigma w - rV = -y$

b.   $V = V(x,y)$; $V(q,y) = 0$, $V_x(\infty,y) < \infty$, $V_y(x,\infty) < \infty$, $V_y(x, -\infty) > -\infty$.

c.   Let $\zeta = \sqrt{(\beta^2 + 2rw^2)}$, $k_2 = -(\beta + \zeta)/w^2$,
$c = (\alpha + k_2\rho\sigma w)/\zeta$. Then

$$V = \left[\frac{y}{r} + \frac{\alpha}{r^2}\right] - \left[\frac{y}{r} + \frac{\alpha}{r^2} + \frac{c(x-q)}{r}\right]\exp[k_2(x - q)]$$

1.9 a.   The values of the primitive securities are given below:

$$Y_1(X) = \frac{1}{r}\{1 - \exp[k_2(X-q)]\}$$

$$Y_2(X) = \left[\frac{X}{r} + \frac{r-\delta}{r^2}\right] - \left[\frac{q}{r} + \frac{r-\delta}{r^2}\right]\exp[k_2(X-q)]$$

$$Y_3(X;c) = k_2\xi\exp[k_1(X-c)] - k_2\xi\exp[k_2(X-q) - k_1(c-q)]$$

$$+ \left(k_1\xi\exp[k_2(X-c)] - k_2\xi\exp[k_1(X-c)] + \frac{1}{r}\right)I_{X>c}$$

$$Y_4(X;c) = B_1\exp[k_1(X-c)] - B_1\exp[k_2(X-q) - k_1(c-q)]$$

$$+ \left(A_1\exp(k_2(X-c)] - B_1\exp[k_1(X-c)] + \frac{X}{r} + \frac{r-\delta}{r^2}\right)I_{X>c}$$

$$k_1, k_2 = [-(r-\delta)\pm\sqrt{[(r-\delta)^2 + 2r\sigma^2]}]/\sigma^2 \quad k_1 > 0 > k_2$$

$$A_1 = \xi[ck_1 + (k_1(r-\delta) - r)/r] \quad B_1 = \xi[ck_2 + (k_2(r-\delta) - r)/r]$$

$$\xi = 1/[r(k_2 - k_1)]$$

b. $D = cY_3 + Y_2 - kY_1 - Y_4 + kY_3$; $E = (1-\theta)(Y_4 - cY_3)$

  $G = \theta(Y_4 - cY_3)$; $T = k(Y_1 - Y_3)$

c. Maximizing $(D + E)$ is equivalent to minimizing $(G + T)$. Take the derivative of either expression with respect to c and q to find the first order conditions for value maximization.

# 2

# Complications of the Basic Paradigm

## Introduction

This chapter enables the student to expand upon the intuition developed in Chapter 1 and shows how to solve many of the problems he or she will encounter. The chapter begins with a taxonomy of frequently occurring differential equations and shows how to solve these equations by substitution or inversion of a Laplace transform. Laplace transform tables can be found in the appendix to the book. The student need not become an expert in transform methods to use the Laplace transforms; several examples are provided.

Because cash flows are separable and asset values may be homogeneous in cash flows, asset valuation can often be made simpler by taking advantage of these properties. The chapter shows how to decompose cash flows to take advantage of these properties and then how to determine the appropriate discount rate for cash flows using a Capital Asset Pricing Model (CAPM) or Arbitrage Pricing Theory (APT) framework. The expected return equation is used to determine the certainty-equivalent growth rate for cash flows; the resulting discount rate is the risk-free rate.

Lastly, the chapter shows how to use valuation techniques recursively, such as when an asset evolves over time into another asset, whose value evolves into another asset, and so on. For some asset-pricing problems, this is the only available valuation technique.

## Frequently Occurring Differential Equations

Why should we worry about partial differential equations (PDEs) in finance? Partial differential equations arise when the value of an asset depends on calendar time and a single state variable, or on multiple state variables. Partial differential equations arise frequently in continuous-time finance. The expression "total return equals capital gain plus cash flow" is itself a PDE, and one that is often used to solve for asset values. The capital gain on an asset V is determined by Itô's Lemma to be dV, as calculated in Chapter 1.

Why should we concentrate on a few types of PDEs? In their 1985 paper, Cox, Ingersoll and Ross (1985a) showed that for a given set of state variables,[1] and assumptions about the behavior of these state variables, all assets traded in the economy satisfy the same differential equation. However, assets may have different cash flows and may satisfy different boundary conditions.[2] Indeed, slightly different boundary conditions or terminal conditions for asset values can have a tremendous impact on asset prices, as we will see in Chapter 3.

Cases I through II on the following pages examine one set of frequently occurring ordinary differential equations (ODEs), and Cases III through IV examine a second set of frequently occurring PDEs. The first set represents time-homogeneous problems with a single state variable. In Case I, the state variable follows arithmetic Brownian motion, and in Case II, the state variable follows geometric Brownian motion. Cases III and IV extend Cases I and II respectively to time inhomogeneous cases, where asset value depends on time (or time to maturity).

When X follows a univariate Itô process, an asset value f(X) depends on the value of X, and there is no explicit termination date for the asset, an ordinary differential equation obtains for the value

---

[1]That is, a set of variables that completely describes the state of an economy.

[2]Boundary conditions place restrictions on asset values when relevant state variables fall outside of a predetermined range.

of the asset. The most common equations contain a nonhomogeneous part and terminal boundary conditions that are linear in X; this section values assets that meet these conditions.

**Case I**     X follows arithmetic Brownian motion, and f = f(X)

In this case, the following differential equation may obtain for the value of f(X):

$$af_{xx} + bf_x + cf = Xd + e$$

where a, b, c, d, and e are constants. Typically, a > 0, c < 0, d < 0 and e < 0. Therefore, $b^2 - 4ac$ will typically be positive. The solution to this equation is given by:

$$f(X) = A_1 \exp(k_1 X) + A_2 \exp(k_2 X) + Xd/c + (ec - bd)/c^2$$

where

$$k_{1,2} = [-b \pm \sqrt{(b^2 - 4ac)}] / [2a], \quad k_1 > k_2$$

Note that if ac < 0, then $k_1 > 0 > k_2$. Boundary conditions determine the value of $A_1$ and $A_2$. It is often the case that as X→∞, $f_x$ must be bounded; if this is true, and ac < 0, then $A_1 = 0$. If, as X→∞ (with ac < 0), either $|V(X)| < ∞$ or $|V_X(X)| < ∞$, then $A_2 = 0$.

**Case II**     X follows geometric Brownian motion, and f = f(X)

In this case, the following differential equation may obtain for the value of f(X):

$$aX^2 f_{xx} + bXf_x + cf = Xd + e$$

The solution is given by:

$$f(X) = A_1 X^{\gamma_1} + A_2 X^{\gamma_2} + \frac{Xd}{b+c} + \frac{e}{c}$$

where $\gamma_{1,2} = [(a - b) \pm \sqrt{\{(b - a)^2 - 4ac\}}] / [2a]$, $\gamma_1 > \gamma_2$. If $ac < 0$ then $\gamma_1 > 0 > \gamma_2$. If $a > 0$ and either $(a + b < 0$ or $-c > b)$ then $\gamma_1 > 1$. Boundary conditions determine the values of $A_1$ and $A_2$. If $f_x$ is bounded as $X \rightarrow \infty$ and $\gamma_1 > 1$, then $A_1 = 0$. If $e = 0$ and $f(0) = 0$, then $A_2 = 0$.

## Example

Consider once again Example B from Chapter 1, but assume we have no guess as to the value of $f(X)$. The boundary conditions require a bounded derivative as $X \rightarrow \infty$ and that $f(0) = 0$, since when X reaches 0, it stays at zero and no more cash flows accrue to the security. The differential equation obtained was:

$$\tfrac{1}{2}\sigma^2 X^2 V_{xx} + \alpha X V_x - rV = -X$$

Therefore, the conditions of Case II are satisfied with $a = \tfrac{1}{2}\sigma^2$, $b = \alpha$, $c = -r$, $d = -1$, and $e = 0$. The solution is given by:

$$f(X) = A_1 X^{\gamma_1} + A_2 X^{\gamma_2} + \frac{Xd}{b+c} + \frac{e}{c}$$

Since $f(0) = 0$, $A_2 = 0$. If it were not the case, $f(X)$ would become unbounded as $X \rightarrow 0$, since $\gamma_2 < 0$. Also, since $f_x$ is bounded, $A_1 = 0$ if $\gamma_1 > 1$, which is satisfied if $\sigma > 0$ and $r > \alpha$. After simplifying, we have

$$f(X) = Xd/(b + c) = -X/(\alpha - r) = X/(r - \alpha).$$

## The Time–Inhomogeneous Cases [f = f(X,τ)]

It is more often true that an asset has a finite life τ, and when it expires, it has a deterministic value such as $f(X,0) = mX + n$. For example, an annuity expires worthless on its expiration date, but a forward contract has the same value as the cash contract at the expiration date.

It is often convenient to reverse the order of time and count backward from τ to 0 instead of forward from 0 to T, as shown below. This implies that $\tau = T - t$, where τ is time to expiration, T is the fixed expiration date, and t is the current time. It also clearly implies that $d\tau = -dt$, so the chain rule of calculus allows us to conclude for any asset value f, that the partial derivative $f_t = -f_\tau$. We shall use this substitution frequently in applying Itô's lemma.

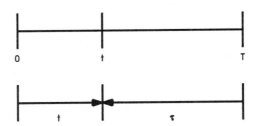

Also, a termination condition for an asset in calendar time is an initial condition for an asset measured in time-to-maturity. This section shows how to value an asset with finite life when X follows arithmetic or geometric Brownian motion; the asset value at termination is assumed to be $f(X,0) = mX + n$.

*A Digression on Laplace Transforms*

Many PDEs involve time passage and are more easily solved with Laplace transforms. By definition, if $f(X,\tau)$ is a function of a variable X and time, then its transform $L_q\{f(X,\tau)\}$ is given as:

$$L_q\{f(X,\tau)\} = \int_0^\infty e^{-qs} f(X,s)ds$$

The equation resembles a continuously discounted present value of cash flows of $f(X,\tau)$, taken at the rate of q. This transformation eliminates time from the function [i.e., $f(X,\tau)$ becomes $g(X)$] and in some cases makes a PDE easier to solve.

Let $g(X) \equiv L_q\{f(X,\tau)\}$. The following properties of $g(X)$ are important in taking transforms of functions $f(X,\tau)$:

1.  Any partial derivative of the transform of a function equals the transform of the partial derivative, except for the time derivative. This applies to second partial derivatives as well:

$$g_X(X) = L_q\{f_X(X,\tau)\}$$

The property can easily be shown by applying Leibniz' rule for differentiation under an integral sign.

2.  The Laplace transform of the time derivative (time = time to maturity) equals the following:

$$L_q\{f_\tau(X,\tau)\} = q\, L_q\{f(X,\tau)\} - f(X,0)$$

The second term in the difference is the terminal value of the security.

3.  The Laplace transform is a linear operator:

$$L\{af(X,\tau) + bg(X,\tau)\} = aL\{f\} + bL\{g\}$$

This applies to the inverse Laplace transform as well. These three properties (and others shown in the appendix) will help you manipulate Laplace transforms to your advantage. Once you have solved a simplified ODE for g(X), use the Laplace transform tables in the appendix to find the reverse transform, f(X,τ), the value of the asset.

**Case III**    X follows arithmetic Brownian motion and f = f(X,τ)

In this case, the following differential equation may obtain for the value of f(X,τ):

$$af_{xx} + bf_x + cf - f_\tau = Xd + e; \; f(X,0) = mX + n.$$

Let $h(X) = L_s\{f(X,\tau)\}$ represent the Laplace transform of f with parameter s. Then the following equation must be satisfied:

$$ah_{xx} + bh_x + (c - s)h = X(d - ms)/s + (e - ns)/s$$

The operations may be checked with the "Digression on Laplace Transforms." The transformation eliminates the time derivative from the PDE.

From Case I we know:

$$h = A_1\exp(k_1 X) + A_2\exp(k_2 X) + X(d - ms)/[s(c - s)]$$
$$+ (e - ns)/[s(c - s)] - b(d - ms)/[s(c - s)^2]$$

where

$$k_{1,2} = [-b \pm \sqrt{\{b^2 - 4a(c - s)\}}] / [2a], \; k_1 > k_2.$$

We normally assume (if a > 0) that s is large enough to make a(c - s) < 0, and therefore $k_1 > 0 > k_2$.

Once again, the values of $A_1$ and $A_2$ are determined by boundary conditions on h, which may be different from boundary conditions on f. To find the value of f, we must invert h using tables of Laplace transforms. Note that $A_1$ and $A_2$ often depend on s; this may make inversion difficult. In many cases, these terms should be expanded into the sum of several fractions involving s in simple ways. If this is possible, the linearity of the inverse transform allows you to find the inverse transform of each component separately, and add or subtract as necessary.

**Case IV**    X follows geometric Brownian motion and $f = f(X,\tau)$

In this case, the following differential equation may obtain for the value of $f(X,\tau)$:

$$aX^2 f_{xx} + bX f_x + cf - f_\tau = Xd + e; \quad f(X,0) = mX + n.$$

Let $h(X) = L_s\{f(X,\tau)\}$ represent the Laplace transform of f with parameter s. Then the following equation must be satisfied:

$$aX^2 h_{xx} + bX h_x + (c - s)h = X(d - ms)/s + (e - ns)/s$$

and from Case II we have:

$$h(X) = A_1 X^{\gamma_1} + A_2 X^{\gamma_2} + \frac{X(d - ms)}{s(b + c - s)} + \frac{e - ns}{s(c - s)}$$

where
$$\gamma_{1,2} = [(a - b) \pm \sqrt{\{(b - a)^2 - 4a(c - s)\}}] / [2a], \gamma_1 > \gamma_2.$$

Again, assume (when $a > 0$) that s is large enough to give the result that $a(c - s) < 0$, and therefore $\gamma_1 > 0 > \gamma_2$.

The values of $A_1$ and $A_2$ are determined by boundary conditions on h, which may be different from boundary conditions on f. To find the value of f, we must invert h using tables of Laplace transforms.

## Example

Consider once again Example B from Chapter 1, but assume the cash flows last for $\tau$ periods only. Then, when the asset expires, $f(X,0) = 0$. We can apply Case IV with the following substitutions:

$$
\begin{array}{ll}
a = \tfrac{1}{2}\sigma^2 & n = 0 \\
b = \alpha & d = -1 \\
c = -r & e = 0 \\
m = 0 &
\end{array}
$$

The solution of the Laplace transform is given by:

$$ h(X) = A_1 X^{\gamma_1} + A_2 X^{\gamma_2} + \frac{X}{s(r - \alpha + s)} $$

The derivative is bounded, so $A_1 = 0$. $h(0) = 0$ (The Laplace transform of 0), so $A_2 = 0$. Using equation 29.3.12 from Abramowitz and Stegun (reproduced in the appendix), we have:

$$ h = X / [(s + a)(s + b)] \text{ with } a = 0 \text{ and } b = r - \alpha $$

(The notation for a and b is chosen to be consistent with the appendix and has nothing to do with the previous definitions of a and b.) We invert h to find:

$$ f(X,\tau) = X[1 - \exp\{-(r - \alpha)\tau\}] / [r - \alpha] $$

Therefore, f is the present value of an annuity with initial level X and growth rate $\alpha$, discounted at the risk-free rate of r.

# Notes on the Separability and Homogeneity of Cash Flows

For the sake of discussion, we consider Case IV but note that the results here can be applied to all problems involving PDEs. This section is most useful when we want to solve a problem for which a similar valuation result is known. We begin by examining the PDE:

$$aX^2f_{xx} + bXf_x + cf - f_\tau = Xd + e; \; f(X,0) = mX + n.$$

We can write f as the sum of two asset values. The first asset, $f_1$, has the continuous cash flows $-(Xd + e)$, but it is worth nothing at maturity; $f_1(X,0) = 0$. The second asset, $f_2$, receives no intermittent cash flows ($d = e = 0$), but it is worth $mX + n$ at maturity. The assets can be further decomposed, as long as the intermediate and terminal values add to the total. For example, $f_1$ can further be broken down into two assets, one that pays $-Xd$ continuously and nothing at maturity, and a second that pays $-e$ continuously and nothing at maturity. To see that this result holds, examine the solution for the Laplace transform of the asset value:

$$h(X) = A_1 X^{\gamma_1} + A_2 X^{\gamma_2} + \frac{X(d - ms)}{s(b + c - s)} + \frac{e - ns}{s(c - s)}$$

There are four cash flow terms, one proportional to d, m, e, and n. The terms may be separated and recombined freely, according to the needs of a particular problem. However, one must be careful to specify the boundary conditions for the necessary cash flows; if a boundary condition applies to the sum of a series of cash flows, it need not apply to every cash flow term.

If an individual cash flow component is multiplied by a constant, the value of that component must be multiplied by the same constant. Also, if there are continuous and discrete cash flows, the asset value may be decomposed to reflect the sources of the cash flows.

We occasionally find the need to value assets for which the cash flows and/or terminal boundary conditions are not linear in X. If the cash flow or boundary condition is piecewise linear, we can solve the PDE in each range and add conditions on the asset values so calculated. For example, if the continuous cash flows are equal to the maximum of X - E and 0, we can solve for the asset value when X > E and when X < E. We note that the same boundary conditions do not apply to each range. However, if V is continuous, we impose a continuity condition at X = E. Furthermore, it may be supposed that V is continuously differentiable or twice continuously differentiable; the derivative $V_x$ (and possibly $V_{xx}$) must also be continuous at X = E.

## The Discount Rate for Financial Assets

We assume no particular arbitrage and/or equilibrium specification, only that the following properties obtain from the model under consideration:

1. There exists a freely traded security, M, such that risk uncorrelated with changes in M is not priced.
2. There are no cash payouts associated with M.
3. M follows geometric Brownian motion with drift $\alpha_m$ and volatility $\sigma_m$.
4. The risk-free rate of interest is constant.

The critical assumption is the first; the second two may be loosened, but are retained for the remainder of this section. The fourth assumption may be loosened, but often at the expense of analytic tractability. We define the beta of a security (X) through its correlation with M:[3]

$$\beta \equiv \rho\sigma_x(X,t)/(X\sigma_m)$$

The terms in the equation are defined below. As in the prior section, we assume that the value of an asset V depends on a stochastic process X and time. The asset has a claim to continuous

---

[3]In a special case of the intertemporal version of the capital asset pricing model (Merton, 1973), $\beta$ reduces to $\beta = \rho\sigma_x \, \sigma_m/\sigma_m^2$, which is the same as the one-period CAPM $\beta$. In this context, M can be interpreted as the market portfolio.

cash payments of g(X,t). A Poisson jump component can be introduced with no difficulty. We assume X follows the general process:

$$dX = \alpha_x(X,t)\ dt + \sigma_x(X,t)\ dZ_x$$

And the index security follows:

$$dM = \alpha_m M\ dt + \sigma_m M\ dZ_m$$

with the correlation defined as:

$$\rho dt = dZ_x dZ_m$$

with dZ representing standard Wiener processes in all cases. This implies (from Chapter 1) that:

$$dZ_x = \rho dZ_m + \sqrt{(1 - \rho^2)} dZ_\varepsilon \text{ and } dZ_m dZ_\varepsilon = 0$$

with the first equality implying equality in distribution. $dZ_\varepsilon$ is a standard Wiener process independent of $dZ_m$.

We begin in the usual fashion:

$$V = V(X,\tau)$$
$$dV = V_x dX + \tfrac{1}{2}V_{xx}dX^2 - V_\tau dt$$
$$= [V_x\alpha_x(X,t) + \tfrac{1}{2}V_{xx}\sigma_x^2(X,t) - V_\tau]dt + V_x\sigma_x(X,t)dZ_x$$

Now form a portfolio that is long one unit of V and h units of the index portfolio:

$$P = V + hM$$

Its law of motion is (from Itô's Lemma):

$$dP = dV + hdM$$

Substituting dV and dM we have:

$$dP = [V_x\alpha_x(X,t) + \tfrac{1}{2}V_{xx}\sigma_x^2(X,t) - V_\tau + h\alpha_m M]dt$$
$$+ V_x\sigma_x(X,t)dZ_x + h\sigma_m MdZ_m$$

Substituting the decomposition of $dZ_x$ and combining terms, we have:

$$dP = [V_x\alpha_x(X,t) + \tfrac{1}{2}V_{xx}\sigma_x^2(X,t) - V_\tau + h\alpha_m M]dt$$
$$+ [V_x\sigma_x(X,t)\rho + h\sigma_m M]dZ_m + V_x\sigma_x(X,t)\sqrt{(1 - \rho^2)}dZ_\varepsilon$$

We choose h to dynamically eliminate the $dZ_m$ term:

$$h = -V_x\sigma_x(X,t)\rho/[\sigma_m M]$$

which implies that:

$$hM = -V_x\beta X$$

The expected return on the hedged portfolio equals the risk-free rate, even though some risks have not been eliminated. By construction (and assumption 1), the residual risk ($dZ_\varepsilon$) is not priced. Therefore, the total return on the hedge portfolio is given by:

$$TR = rP\,dt = r(V + hM) = E[dP] + g(X,t)dt = ECG + ECF$$

$$r(V - V_x\beta X) = V_x\alpha_x(X,t) + \tfrac{1}{2}V_{xx}\sigma_x^2(X,t) - V_\tau - V_x\alpha_m\beta X + g(X,t)$$

$$-g(X,t) = \tfrac{1}{2}V_{xx}\sigma_x^2(X,t) + V_x X\left[\frac{\alpha_x(X,t)}{X} - \beta(\alpha_m - r)\right] - rV - V_\tau$$

The term in brackets may be interpreted as the certainty-equivalent growth rate (CEQ) of the X process. The actual growth rate is $\alpha_x$, and the $\beta$ term reduces the actual growth rate until risk-free discounting (rV) is possible. In the special case where X follows geometric Brownian motion, the CEQ growth rate reduces to a constant, $\alpha^* \equiv \alpha_x - \beta(\alpha_m - r)$. See Constantinides (1978) for a generalization. In this view of asset pricing, we adjust the growth rate of the underlying process and calculate expected value as if preferences were neutral.

When X follows geometric Brownian motion, we need only substitute $\alpha^*$ for $\alpha_x$ in the valuation equation. As long as the boundary conditions are unaffected by the substitution, the solution will take the same form in risk-averse and risk-neutral economies. The valuation results of Chapter 1 and earlier in Chapter 2 may be reinterpreted using this new certainty-equivalent growth rate in risk-averse economies.

## Example

Suppose that X itself is a traded asset with no cash flows and that X follows a geometric Brownian motion process. Then the certainty equivalent growth rate of X, $\alpha^*$, must be identical to the riskless rate of interest, r. Therefore, from the value of $\alpha^*$, we have:

$$\alpha_X = r + \beta(\alpha_m - r)$$

This is the expected return equation for the capital asset pricing model (or a special case of the single factor APT).

## Example

Suppose X follows geometric Brownian motion with drift $\alpha$ and volatility $\sigma$. X is correlated with an index portfolio M; $dZ_x dZ_m = \rho dt$. Risk uncorrelated with M has no price. (M is defined on page 43.) An asset V promises to pay the contemporaneous value of X in $\tau$ periods. What is the value of V?

We first derive the PDE:

$$\tfrac{1}{2}\sigma^2 X^2 V_{xx} + \alpha^* X V_x - rV - V_\tau = 0$$

subject to the three boundary conditions: $V(X,0) = X$, $V(0,\tau) = 0$, $V_x(X,\tau) < \infty$. The $\alpha^*$ was defined earlier. The PDE satisfies Case IV with:

$$
\begin{array}{ll}
a = \tfrac{1}{2}\sigma^2 & \qquad e = 0 \\
b = \alpha^* & \qquad m = 1 \\
c = -r & \qquad n = 0 \\
d = 0 &
\end{array}
$$

The last two boundary conditions imply that $A_1 = A_2 = 0$, so $h = X/[s + r - \alpha^*]$. Taking the Laplace transform inverse (29.3.8), we see that $g = X \exp[-(r - \alpha^*)\tau]$. This is the continuously discounted present value of a risk-adjusted expected future value of X.

### Extensions

For multifactor models, if the factor risks can be eliminated and the residual risk diversified, we can calculate the certainty-equivalent growth rate in the same manner; the treatment is symmetric to that of the single-factor case. The hedge portfolio is calculated to eliminate all factor risks.

## Recursive Techniques in Asset Valuation

In some cases, an asset changes its character through time. Consider a simple asset that gives its bearer the right to receive the $k^{th}$ cash flow in an infinite stochastic sequence. The occurrence of each cash flow follows a Poisson arrival process. At the time that the first cash flow occurs, the asset that used to have claim to the $k^{th}$ cash flow of a series now has claim to the $k - 1^{st}$ cash flow of an infinite stochatic series. Let $V_k$ represent the value of a security giving its bearer the right to the $k^{th}$ cash flow of a sequence, and assume that the cash flow size is determined by the contemporaneous level of X, which follows geometric Brownian motion. Then, at every instant, with probability $\lambda dt$, the value of the asset might jump by $(V_{k-1} - V_k)$. The partial differential equation for the asset value appears below: (similar to Example D from Chapter 1, but modified to allow for non-diversifiable risk)

$$\tfrac{1}{2}\sigma^2 X^2 V_{kxx} + \alpha^* X V_{kx} - r V_k - V_{k\tau} = -\lambda(V_{k-1} - V_k) \qquad k = 1,2,...$$
$$V_0 = X$$

The k subscript of V is an index, and the x subscript indicates a partial derivative. Since the claim is perpetual, $V_{k\tau} = 0$. $V_0$ is defined to be equal to X since $V_1$ jumps to X when the Poisson event occurs. In Chapter 1, we saw that $V_1$ equals $X/[1 + \gamma]$, where $\gamma = (r - \alpha^*)/\lambda$. Substituting this expression, we can solve for $V_2 = X/[1 + \gamma]^2$, and in general, $V_k = X/[1 + \gamma]^k$. The specifics of the derivation are left as an exercise to the reader.

Chapter 2 begins to undertake some of the most difficult problems in continuous time financial theory. Many students can derive the PDEs for asset values, but fail to complete the circle and solve for asset values. This chapter is intended to lower the solution hurdle by providing solutions for four commonly occurring ODEs and PDEs and by discussing the Laplace transform solution method. Of course, there are many methods to solve PDEs; we used guesswork in Chapter 1 and the Laplace transform in Chapter 2. Advanced students may use Fourier transforms and even numerical methods to value these securities.

We saw how to value assets in the presence of risk. We substitute the certainty-equivalent growth rate for all the relevant state variables, calculate expected payoffs, and discount at the risk-free rate. This point is elegantly presented in Constantinides (1978). No matter what equilibrium or arbitrage model you employ, this approach can be used to find the asset value. The only difficulty is finding out how to transform the actual growth rate into its certainty equivalent.

Finally, we analyzed situations where recursive valuation is required. When the character of an asset changes through time, the methods of this section can be used to value the asset. Having finished this chapter, you should now know how to value all sorts of claims to cash flows in continuous time.

# Exercises

Unless stated otherwise, assume that all risks are diversifiable and the risk-free rate of interest is constant and equal to r. Assume the drift of X is α and the volatility is σ.

2.1   The level of a continuous index, X, follows geometric Brownian motion. A security V receives cash flows of CX dt for τ periods, where C is a constant.

   a.   Derive the partial differential equation for the value of the asset.

   b.   How many boundary conditions are required to value the asset? What are the appropriate boundary conditions?

   c.   Find the value of the security.

   d.   Conduct comparative statics for r and the drift and volatility parameters. (Calculate and sign the derivatives of V with respect to the parameters of the model.)

2.2   A discount bond pays XD after τ periods pass, where X follows geometric Brownian motion, and D is a constant.

   a.   Write the partial differential equation for this asset.

   b.   State the boundary conditions.

   c.   Find the value of the asset.

   d.   Conduct comparative statics analysis.

2.3   An entrepreneurial finance student decides to create a portfolio that includes both securities in (2.1) and (2.2).

   a.   Provide an economic interpretation for this asset.

   b.   What is the value of this asset?

   c.   Under what conditions is the value additive?

   d.   What are the comparative statics?

2.4    Specialize your result in (2.3) to a risk-free fixed coupon–paying bond. The coupon payment, Cdt, is expressed as a fraction (c) of face value D, a fixed dollar amount. If we interpret X as a price index, then we can think of the result in (2.3) as the value of an inflation-protected bond, and this special case as a noninflation-protected bond.

    a.    What is the value of the (nonprotected) risk-free coupon bond?

    b.    What stochastic process does the nominal (nonprotected) bond price follow? The protected bond price? (*HINT: Calculate total return in each case including cash flows.*)

    c.    At what nominal coupon rate would an investor be indifferent between holding an inflation-protected bond, and a nonprotected bond?

2.5    Assume that the security in problem 2.1 does not pay the cash flow for a fixed time τ, but instead pays X dt until a Poisson event occurs with probability λ dt. It then pays a fixed amount D and nothing thereafter. If τ periods pass before the event occurs, however, the asset expires worthless.

    a.    What partial differential equation does the asset value satisfy?

    b.    What are the boundary conditions?

    c.    Value the asset.

    d.    Conduct comparative statics analysis.

2.6    Let X follow a general continuous-time stochastic process. A security V pays the contemporaneous level of X in τ periods. That is, there are no cash flows to V, but after τ periods pass, the payment to V will be the same as the level of X.

    a.    What partial differential equation must be satisfied by V?

b. Suppose X follows arithmetic Brownian motion with drift $\alpha$ and volatility $\sigma$. What boundary conditions must V satisfy? What is the solution for V?

c. Suppose X follows a mean–reverting square–root process with speed of adjustment $\kappa$, long–run mean $\mu$, and volatility $\sigma$. What boundary conditions must V satisfy? What is the solution for V? *(HINT: The solution to the Laplace transform is linear in X.)*

2.7 Let X follow a mean–reverting square root process with speed of adjustment $\kappa$, long–run mean $\mu$, and volatility $\sigma$. A security V pays Xdt continuously for $\tau$ periods.

a. What PDE must be satisfied?

b. What are the boundary conditions?

c. What is the solution for the asset value?

2.8 Suppose a government sets up a social security system. Every individual pays the continuous, constant amount C dt until some event (retirement or disability) occurs with probability $\lambda_1$ dt. At that time, the individual is paid an annuity of X dt continuously until some second event (death) occurs with probability $\lambda_2$ dt. At that time, the security becomes worthless. Assume that X follows geometric Brownian motion.

a. What is the value of this asset to an individual? (Derive the PDE and state the boundary conditions.)

b. What is the value of C such that the value of the social security contract to the individual is zero?

c. What does the comparative statics analysis suggest?

2.9 A security pays Xdt continuously for $\tau$ periods, where X follows arithmetic Brownian motion.

a. What partial differential equation does the asset's value satisfy?

b.   What are the boundary conditions?

c.   Find the value of the asset. (*HINT: After finding the Laplace transform, use a partial fraction technique to simplify the denominator. Write $1/[s(s + r)^2]$ as $A/[s(s + r)] + B/(s + r)^2 + C/(s + r) + D/s$, and solve for A,B,C, and D. This facilitates the inversion process.*)

d.   Calculate the partial derivatives and verify that the original partial differential equation and boundary conditions are satisfied.

2.10   A Poisson process determines the timing of a potentially infinite sequence of cash flows. The security with claims to these cash flows has a finite life $\tau$. The intensity of the arrival process is $\lambda$. When a cash flow arrives, its level is given by X, which follows arithmetic Brownian motion. Arrivals after $\tau$ periods do not cause cash flows to occur.

a.   What is the value of a claim to the first cash flow in the sequence?

b.   What is the value of a claim to the second cash flow in the sequence?

c.   What is the value of all of the cash flows? How does the value compare to that of a perpetuity of Xdt? An annuity of Xdt?

2.11   Repeat exercise 2.10 if X follows geometric Brownian motion.

2.12   (From Cox, Ingersoll and Ross, 1985b.) Suppose the short-term interest rate follows a square-root mean-reverting process:

$$dr = \kappa(\theta - r)dt + \sigma\sqrt{r}\, dZ$$

A discount bond pays $1 after $\tau$ periods and makes no intermediate cash payments.

    a. Describe the dynamics of the short-term interest rate process.

    b. Let $P = P(r,\tau)$ represent the price of the discount bond. What PDE must this price satisfy?

    c. What are the boundary conditions?

    d. Value the bond. *(HINT: Let $P(r,\tau) = A(\tau)exp[rB(\tau)]$ and separate the variables in the PDE.)*

    e. What stochastic process does the yield of the bond follow?

2.13 (Advanced) Suppose there are n mortgages in a pool. Each mortgage pays a fixed coupon at a contract rate of Cdt until a Poisson event (with constant intensity $\lambda$) occurs, at which time the balance of the mortgage is paid. The term of the mortgage is $\tau$ periods. The balance of the mortgage is taken as the present value of the remaining payments at the contracted interest rate. The $k^{th}$ mortgage to prepay is termed prepayment k, and contingent claims are sold that give the bearers the right to receive all the cash flows from the $k^{th}$ mortgage to prepay. Of course, the identity of the $k^{th}$ prepayment is unknown at time 0.

    a. What is the relationship between the initial loan balance, the loan payment, and the balance of the mortgage at an arbitrary time point t?

    b. Describe the system of differential equations the individual prepayments satisfy.

    c. What is the value of the first prepayment?

    d. What is the value of the $k^{th}$ prepayment?

2.14 (Advanced) Suppose X follows geometric Brownian motion. An investment banker wishes to divide X into two parts. The first part pays Min(X,E)dt continuously for $\tau$ periods. The second part pays Max(X - E,0)dt continuously for $\tau$ periods. *(HINT: Parts a and b can be solved relatively easily by imposing the correct continuity restrictions. Parts c and d are more difficult and may require substantially more calculation.)*

a. Let τ→∞. Show the PDEs that must be satisfied by the first and second parts. State the boundary conditions.

b. Value the first and second parts when τ→∞.

c. Repeat part a. for the finitely-lived security.

d. Repeat part b. for the finitely-lived security.

## Solutions to Exercises

2.1 a. $V = V(X,\tau)$; $\frac{1}{2}\sigma^2X^2V_{XX} + \alpha XV_X - rV - V_\tau = -CX$

   b. 3 boundary conditions; $V(0,\tau) = V(X,0) = 0$ and $V_X(\infty,\tau)<\infty$

   c. $h = CX/[s(s + r - \alpha)]$; use (29.3.12)
      $V = CX(1 - \exp[-(r - \alpha)\tau])/(r - \alpha)$

   d. $V_r < 0$, $V_\alpha > 0$, $V_\sigma = 0$, $V_X > 0$, $V_\tau > 0$.

2.2 a. $V = V(X,\tau)$; $\frac{1}{2}\sigma^2X^2V_{XX} + \alpha XV_X - rV - V_\tau = 0$

   b. $V(0,\tau) = 0$, $V_X(\infty,\tau) < \infty$, and $V(X,0) = XD$

   c. $h = XDs/[s(s + r - \alpha)]$; use (29.3.13)
      $V = XD\exp[-(r - \alpha)\tau]$

   d. $V_r < 0$, $V_\alpha > 0$, $V_\sigma = 0$, $V_X > 0$, $V_\tau < 0$.

2.3 a. The sum of (2.1) and (2.2) might represent an indexed bond; both coupons and principal payments are tied to the same index X.

   b. The value is the sum of its components.

   c. The boundary conditions (for state variable X) are unaffected by the combination of the two assets.

   d. Same as 2.2.d, except that $V_\tau$ has the same sign as $r - C/D$.

**2.4**    a.   Let $X = X_0 = 1$ be normalized to one. To remain constant, $\alpha = \sigma = 0$. In this case, $dX = 0$. As a consequence, $V = D[c/r + (1 - c/r)\exp[-r\tau]]$.

      b.   The total (nonprotected) return process, including cash flows, follows:

$$d(TR) = \{cD(1 - \exp[-r\tau]) + rD\exp[-r\tau]\}dt = rVdt$$

The protected total return follows:

$$d(TR) =$$
$$\{(r - \alpha)V + \alpha XD\exp[-(r - \alpha)\tau][1 - c/(r - \alpha)]\}dt$$
$$+ \sigma V dZ$$

      c.   In order for both bonds to be priced at par, the rate for the nonprotected bond is $c = r$ and for the protected bond, $c = r - \alpha$. In other words, Fisher's rule for the calculation of the nominal rate of interest holds exactly in continuous time: In a risk–neutral economy, the nominal rate of interest equals the real rate of interest plus the expected rate of price appreciation.

**2.5**    a.   $\tfrac{1}{2}\sigma^2 X^2 V_{XX} + \alpha X V_X - rV - V_\tau = -\{X + \lambda(D - V)\}$

      b.   $V(0,\tau) = V(X,0) = 0; \; V_X(\infty,\tau) < \infty$

      c.   $h = X/[s(s + r + \lambda - \alpha)] + \lambda D/[s(s + r + \lambda)]$   (29.3.12)

         $V = X\{1 - \exp[-(r + \lambda - \alpha)\tau]\}/(r + \lambda - \alpha) +$
            $\lambda D\{1 - \exp[-(r + \lambda)\tau]\}/(r + \lambda)$

      d.   $V_\lambda$ is ambiguous; other partial derivatives have the same sign as problem 2.1.

**2.6**    a.   $\tfrac{1}{2}\sigma^2(X,\tau)V_{XX} + \alpha(X,\tau)V_X - rV - V_\tau = 0; \; V(X,0) = X$

      b.   $|V_X(\pm\infty)| < \infty; \; V = (X + \alpha\tau)\exp[-r\tau]$

      c.   $h = (X - \mu)/(s + r + \kappa) + \mu/(s + r);$

         $V = (X - \mu)\exp[-(r + \kappa)\tau] + \mu\exp[-r\tau]$

2.7   a.   $\frac{1}{2}\sigma^2 X V_{XX} + \kappa(\mu - X)V_X - rV - V_\tau = -X$; $V(X,0) = 0$

b.   $V_X(\infty,\tau) < \infty$; $V_X(0,\tau) < \infty$

c.   $V = (X - \mu)(1 - \exp[-(r + \kappa)\tau])/(r + \kappa)$
$+ \mu(1 - \exp[-r\tau])/r$

2.8   a.   Begin by valuing the security contingent upon the $\lambda_1$ event having occurred: the PDE is:

$$\frac{1}{2}\sigma^2 X^2 V_{XX} + \alpha X V_X - rV - V_\tau = -\{X + \lambda_2(0 - V)\}.$$

The Case II solution is $V = X/(r + \lambda_2 - \alpha)$. The PDE that must be satisfied now is:

$$\frac{1}{2}\sigma^2 X^2 V_{XX} + \alpha X V_X - rV - V_\tau =$$
$$- \{-C + \lambda_1[X/(r + \lambda_2 - \alpha) - V].$$

The new Case II solution is:

$$V = \lambda_1 X/[(r + \lambda_1 - \alpha)(r + \lambda_2 - \alpha)] - C/(r + \lambda_1)$$

b.   $C = \lambda_1 X(r + \lambda_1)/[(r + \lambda_1 - \alpha)(r + \lambda_2 - \alpha)$

2.9   a.   $\frac{1}{2}\sigma^2 V_{XX} + \alpha V_X - rV - V_\tau = -X$; $V(X,0) = 0$

b.   $|V_X(\pm\infty,\tau)| < \infty$

c.   $A = 0$, $B = -1/r$, $C = -1/r^2$, $D = 1/r^2$
$V = (X + \alpha/r)(1 - \exp[-r\tau])/r - \alpha\tau\exp[-r\tau]/r$

2.10  a.   The first payment in the sequence is worth:

$$\lambda\left(X + \frac{\alpha}{r+\lambda}\right)\left(\frac{1 - \exp[-(r+\lambda)\tau]}{r+\lambda}\right) - \lambda\left(\frac{\alpha}{r+\lambda}\right)\tau\exp[-r\,\tau]$$

b.   Left to reader.

  c. The value of all the payments is proportional to an annuity of Xdt.

2.11 a. Define $\gamma = (r - \alpha)/\lambda$;
    then $V = X(1 - \exp[-\lambda(1 + \gamma)\tau])/(1 + \gamma)$

  b. $V_2 = V_1/(1 + \gamma) - \lambda\tau\{X\exp[-(r + \lambda - \alpha)\tau]\}/(1 + \gamma)$

  c. The value is equivalent to that of an annuity of $\lambda X dt$ for $\tau$ periods.

2.12 a. The short–run interest rate tends to a long–run value of $\theta$ but is beset with disturbances proportional to the square root of the level of the process. The speed of adjustment determines how quickly (on average) the short rate will revert to the long–run mean. Since there is no steady state, it would be relevant to calculate the average time it takes the short rate to get to $(r + \theta)/2$.

  b. $\frac{1}{2}\sigma^2 r P_{rr} + \kappa(\theta - r)P_r - rP - P_\tau = 0$

  c. $P(r,0) = P(0,\tau) = 1;\ P(\infty,\tau) = 0$

2.13 a. $B(\tau) = C(1 - \exp[-\rho\tau])/\rho$ for all $\tau$; equals loan balance at origination.

  b. $P_k = P_k(r,\lambda j,\tau)$; k represents prepayment number, other subscripts represent partial derivatives:

$$rP_k = -P_{k\tau} + \lambda j[P_{k-1}(r,\lambda(j - 1),\tau) - P_k] + C$$
$$k = 1\,..\,j,\ j = 1\,..\,n$$
$$P_0(r,\lambda(j - 1),\tau) = B(\tau)\quad j = 2\,..\,n$$
$$\Sigma_j P_k(r,\lambda j,\tau) = jP_1(r,\lambda,\tau)\qquad j = 1\,..\,n$$
$$P_k(r,\lambda j,0) = 0\qquad k = 1\,..\,j,\ j = 1\,..\,n$$

  c. Left to reader, this is a special case of d.

d.

$$P_k(r,\lambda n,\tau) = \frac{c}{r}\left(1 - e^{-r\tau}\right) + \frac{c(r - \rho)}{r\rho}\left(\frac{\lambda n}{r + \lambda n}\right)^k \Phi(k,r + \lambda n,\tau)$$

$$+ \frac{ce^{-r\tau}}{r}\Phi(k,\lambda n,\tau) - \frac{ce^{-\rho\tau}}{\rho}\left(\frac{\lambda n}{r + \lambda n - \rho}\right)^k \Phi(k,r + \lambda n,\tau)$$

where

$$\Phi(\alpha,\beta,\tau) = \int_0^\tau \frac{x^{\alpha-1}e^{-\beta x}\beta^\alpha}{\Gamma(\alpha)}dx$$

$$\Gamma(\alpha) = \int_0^\infty s^{\alpha-1}e^{-s}ds$$

$\Gamma(\alpha)$ is the gamma function, and $\Phi(\alpha,\beta,\tau)$ is the cumulative distribution function of the gamma distribution function. When $\alpha = 1$, the gamma reduces to an exponential distribution.

2.14 We value the security that pays Max(X - E,0) for a finite time period. The remaining exercises are left to the reader.

Let $v = m/a$, $b_1 = \ln(X/E)/(\sigma\sqrt{\tau}) + \sigma v\sqrt{\tau}$,
$b_2 = b_1 - 2\sigma v\sqrt{\tau}$.

$d_1 = [\ln(X/E) + (\alpha + \tfrac{1}{2}\sigma^2)\tau]/[\sigma\sqrt{\tau}]$; $d_2 = d_1 - \sigma\sqrt{\tau}$

$A = [r - \alpha(\gamma - v)]/[2\delta rv]$; $B = [\alpha(\gamma + v)-r]/[2\delta rv]$

$m^2 = r + a^2\gamma^2$; $a^2 = \tfrac{1}{2}\sigma^2$; $\gamma = [a^2 - \alpha]/\sigma^2$; $\delta = r - \alpha$

Then if X < E, we have:

$$W = EA(X/E)^{r+v}N(b_1) + EB(X/E)^{r-v}N(b_2)$$
$$- \frac{X\exp[-\delta\tau]}{\delta}N(d_1) + \frac{E\exp[-r\tau]}{r}N(d_2)$$

if $X > E$, we have:

$$W = \frac{X}{\delta} - \frac{E}{r}$$
$$- EA(X/E)^{r+v}N(-b_1) - EB(X/E)^{r-v}N(-b_2)$$
$$- \frac{X\exp[-\delta\tau]}{\delta}N(d_1) + \frac{E\exp[-r\tau]}{r}N(d_2)$$

The solution is continuous and continuously differentiable at $X = E$.

# 3

# The Valuation of Derivative Securities

## Introduction

We define a **derivative security** as one whose value depends exclusively on a fixed set of asset values and time. We can value derivatives on nontraded variables in an equilibrium setting and derivatives on traded securities in an arbitrage setting.

After understanding the intuition of stochastic cash flows, derivative securities are easier to analyze. Historically, one of the first applications of continuous methods was made to derivative securities, most notably by Black and Scholes (1973). The chapter begins with a Black–Scholes type derivation of the value of a derivative security, with the twist that $\pi$ represents the proportion of the value of a contract paid in cash. For options the proportion is $\pi = 1$, and for pure forward contracts, $\pi = 0$. The partial differential equations for these two asset classes are the same; only the boundary conditions vary. The first parts of this chapter lay out the general arbitrage pricing result and show how to find the value of forward contracts and options using the methods presented in the text until this point.

Arbitrage valuation for derivative securities relies on the free tradability of the underlying asset; this critical assumption is never violated in this chapter. In the absence of a freely traded underlying security (e.g., the value of a piece of land on which a call option is written), an equilibrium approach may be used. For convenience, we also generally assume that the risk-free interest rate is constant;

in some cases, the results can be easily extended to account for stochastic interest rates.[1]

Later, the chapter presents a basic equilibrium result and shows the impact of this result on the differential equation for asset values. The results are then applied to the valuation of options and forward contracts. Lastly, the chapter discusses the problem of time-dependent boundary conditions. In many cases, these problems cannot be solved in closed form, so the researcher usually relies on numerical evaluation techniques.

## A General Arbitrage Valuation Result

In this section we examine the pricing of a derivative security, given the valuation of a primary security. By our definition, a derivative security's value depends at most upon the value of the primary security and time. Even if the primary security is valued using equilibrium methods, the derivative security may be valued using arbitrage techniques. If the underlying security is not freely traded or has some rate of return shortfall, then equilibrium considerations must be used to price the derivative security. In addition, a derivative security's value may depend on several primary securities; this extension is straightforward once one understands the basic methodology.

We assume a general continuous process for the primary security (X):

$$dX = \alpha(X,t)\, dt + \sigma(X,t)\, dZ$$

where dZ is a standard Wiener process. The derivative security, V, is written as a function of X and t only; therefore we can write:

---

[1]For options and forward contracts, stochastic interest rates may be accounted for by substituting B for $\exp(-r\tau)$, where B is the price of a T-Bill per \$1 face value maturing on the same date as the derivative contract.

$$dV = V_x dX + \tfrac{1}{2} V_{xx} dX^2 - V_\tau dt$$

We assume that a proportion of the value, $\pi$, must be deposited in a margin account. If securities can be used for margin, then $\pi = 0$; if full cash is paid, then $\pi = 1$. We construct an arbitrage portfolio, $P = V + hX$, and note that:

$$dP = dV + hdX = (V_x + h)dX + \tfrac{1}{2} V_{xx} dX^2 - V_\tau dt$$

To **completely** eliminate the risk of this hedge portfolio, we let $h = -V_x$. Because the hedge portfolio bears no risk, $dP$ must be proportional to the investment in the hedge portfolio, $\pi V - V_x X$; $rP dt = r(\pi V - V_x X)$. Therefore, we have:

$$\tfrac{1}{2}\sigma^2(X,t)V_{xx} + rXV_x - \pi rV - V_\tau = 0$$

which is a general arbitrage valuation equation for derivative securities. The boundary conditions will determine the actual valuation equation. Especially noteworthy is the fact that $\alpha(X,t)$ does not affect the valuation; as long as X is priced correctly, the effects of $\alpha(X,t)$ are summarized completely in the value of X.

# Arbitrage Valuation of Forward Contracts and Options

## The Forward Contract

A **forward contract** provides a nonrevokable agreement between two parties that a particular asset will be exchanged at some time in the future, for a price agreed upon today. In theory, no cash changes hands today; parties may be required to deposit margin (possibly in the form of marketable securities) to ensure contract performance. For now, we assume $\pi$ is arbitrary, but traditionally, one assumes that $\pi = 0$ for forward contracts.

Let X represent the price of the primary security or the underlying commodity, whichever interpretation is appropriate. We assume there are no carrying costs, dividends, convenience yield, or anything that interferes with the free and continuous trading of the primary security. We assume that X follows geometric Brownian motion; $\alpha(X,t) = \alpha X$, and $\sigma(X,t) = \sigma X$. The boundary conditions for the forward contract require that $V(X,0) = X$, $V(0,\tau) = 0$ and $V_x(X,\tau) < \infty$ for $\tau < \infty$. The first boundary condition obtains because a contract to exchange immediately must have a price equal to the price of the underlying contract. The second boundary condition obtains because zero is an absorbing barrier of X; once X becomes zero, it stays at zero, so the price of the forward contract must be zero. The last boundary condition insures that the hedge ratio be finite; this permits elimination of underlying security risks.

The partial differential equation reduces to:

$$\tfrac{1}{2}\sigma^2 X^2 V_{xx} + rXV_x - \pi rV - V_\tau = 0; \quad V(X,0) = X$$

which satisfies the conditions of Case IV in Chapter 2. Therefore, we have:

| | | | | |
|---|---|---|---|---|
| a | = | $\tfrac{1}{2}\sigma^2$ | e = | 0 |
| b | = | r | m = | 1 |
| c | = | $-\pi r$ | n = | 0 |
| d | = | 0 | | |

The LaPlace transform of V is equal to

$$h(X) = A_1 X^{\gamma_1} + A_2 X^{\gamma_2} + \frac{X(d - ms)}{s(b + c - s)} + \frac{e - ns}{s(c - s)}$$

The second boundary condition forces $A_2 = 0$, and the third boundary condition forces $A_1 = 0$. After making substitutions:

$$h = X/[s - (1 - \pi)r]$$

which upon taking the inverse LaPlace transform yields:

$$V = X \exp[r(1 - \pi)\tau]$$

Under these assumptions, the agreed price of the forward contract is greater than the spot price as long as $\pi < 1$. The hedge ratio, $V_x = V/X$, is greater than or equal to one and approaches unity as time to maturity approaches zero. Therefore, a perfectly hedged position holds one forward contract and is short $V/X$ units of the spot commodity.

## The European Call Option Contract

A **European call option** contract allows its owner to purchase one unit of the underlying commodity at a fixed price of E, $\tau$ periods in the future. Or, the owner of the call option may decide not to exercise if the price of the underlying commodity is less than E. Therefore, the value of a call option in $\tau$ periods is X - E if X > E and 0 if X < E; $V(X,0) = \text{Max}(X - E,0)$. Furthermore, we have $V(0,\tau) = 0$ and $V_x(X,\tau) < \infty$. Normally, the price of the option is paid in full; $\pi = 1$. A European call option satisfies the derivative security condition if its value, V, can be written as a function of the underlying security, X, and time only. If we assume that X follows geometric Brownian motion, then we can write the partial differential equation for section 3.1:

$$\tfrac{1}{2}V_{xx}\sigma^2X^2 + rXV_x - rV - V_\tau = 0; \quad V(X,0) = \text{Max}(X - E,0)$$

The PDE meets the conditions of Case IV, with:

| | | | | | |
|---|---|---|---|---|---|
| a | = | $\tfrac{1}{2}\sigma^2$ | e | = | 0 |
| b | = | r | m | = | {1,0} |
| c | = | -r | n | = | {-E,0} |
| d | = | 0 | | | |

We have two equations for the LaPlace transform, one when X > E and the second when X < E:

$$h(X) = A_1 X^{\gamma_1} + A_2 X^{\gamma_2} + \frac{X(d - ms)}{s(b + c - s)} + \frac{e - ns}{s(c - s)}$$

The equations are identical except for the constants $A_1$ and $A_2$ and the constants m and n. In the high case (X > E), $A_1 = 0$ because of the boundedness of the derivative. In the low case, $A_2 = 0$ because the option value approaches zero as the stock price goes to zero. The equations reduce to:

$$h(X > E) = A_2 X^{\gamma_2} + X/s - E/[s + r]$$

$$h(X < E) = A_1 X^{\gamma_1}$$

The values of $A_1$ and $A_2$ are determined by additional boundary conditions. In particular, we require continuity of the option pricing function at X = E, and continuity of the first derivative (with respect to X). In this example, continuity of the second derivative is guaranteed. The continuity requirements are met if

$$A_1 = \left[ \frac{\gamma_2}{s + r} - \frac{(\gamma_2 - 1)}{s} \right] \frac{E^{1 - \gamma_1}}{\gamma_1 - \gamma_2}$$

$$A_2 = \left[ \frac{\gamma_1}{s + r} - \frac{(\gamma_1 - 1)}{s} \right] \frac{E^{1 - \gamma_2}}{\gamma_1 - \gamma_2}$$

The inverse LaPlace transforms are the same in the high and low cases. In particular, we note a useful LaPlace transform:

$$\mathcal{L}_s \left\{ \exp(f\tau) N\left[ \frac{d + b\tau}{c\sqrt{\tau}} \right] \right\} = \frac{1}{2} \exp(-ak) \frac{\exp\left(-k\sqrt{s - f + a^2}\right)}{\sqrt{s - f + a^2}\,(a + \sqrt{s - f + a^2})}$$

where $N(\cdot)$ is the cumulative normal distribution function, $a = -b/[c\sqrt{2}]$ and $k = -d\sqrt{2}/c$. The original function, after much algebraic manipulation, reduces to:

$$V(X,\tau) = XN(d_1) - E\exp(-r\tau)N(d_2)$$

The parameter $d_1 = [\ln(X/E) + (r + \tfrac{1}{2}\sigma^2)\tau]/[\sigma\sqrt{\tau}]$, and $d_2 = d_1 - \sigma\sqrt{\tau}$. The hedge ratio, $V_x$ reduces to $N(d_1)$, since $XN'(d_1) - E\exp(-r\tau)N'(d_2) = 0$. $N'(z)$ is the standard normal density function evaluated at z. As long as $(r + \tfrac{1}{2}\sigma^2) > 0$, the hedge ratio approaches 1 as $\tau\rightarrow\infty$. As $\tau\rightarrow0$, the hedge ratio approaches 1 if $X > E$ and 0 if $X < E$.

## An Equilibrium Valuation Result

We now consider a case where the rate of return on the underlying security is out of equilibrium; the certainty-equivalent rate of return is below the risk-free rate (r) by an amount ($\delta$).

How can the underlying security earn a return inconsistent with equilibrium? Although the language is suggestive, this may not be the case at all. For example, suppose a stock follows geometric Brownian motion but continuously pays a dividend that is proportional to the level of the stock price. The holders of the stock, of course, earn an equilibrium rate of return. The shareholders have claim to the dividends, however, unlike the holders of options written against the stock. Therefore, option holders see the price of the stock following a process that earns inferior returns. They must price the option accordingly. For stocks that pay dividends quarterly, the assumption that dividends are paid continuously may create significant divergences between market and model prices. However, for options written against stock indexes, the proportional continuous dividend assumption is more appropriate.

In futures markets, the cost-of-carry plays the role of a negative dividend. For those who hold the underlying commodity against which a futures contract is written, storage, maintenance and spoilage costs must be incurred. If the sum of these costs is approximately proportional to the level of the cash commodity price, then the results in this section can be used to price the futures contract. Others have argued that holders of the cash commodities earn a convenience yield, a bonus for (locally) monopolistic power in times of shortfalls. Once again, if the convenience yield is proportional to the cash commodity price, the methods of this section can be used to price the futures contract.

As a final application, consider an option written against a futures contract. We valued an option on a stock in the last section, on the assumption that the stock paid no dividends and earned a rate of return consistent with equilibrium. A futures contract (with no initial cash investment) appears in this context to earn a below-equilibrium rate of return, lower by the amount r. Therefore, an option on a futures contract may be priced by assuming $\delta = r$.

To see why futures earn a lower rate of return, consider that the total return on any asset depends on two components, a "waiting" component and a "worrying" component [in the CAPM, $r_i = r_f$ (Wait) $+ \beta(r_m - r_f)$ (Worry)]. If marketable securities can be deposited as margin, then futures has no waiting component, so the return is lower by an amount $r_f$. This is the same effect as a stock paying a dividend. The results in this section can be traced to Black (1976) and McDonald and Siegel (1984).

In the event of a rate-of-return shortfall, the standard techniques we have developed until this point can be used to show that the following equation holds for the value of the derivative security:

$$\tfrac{1}{2}\sigma^2 X^2 V_{xx} + (r - \delta)XV_x - \pi r V - V_\tau = 0$$

We consider the substitution $Y = X\exp[-\delta\tau]$, and let $V(X,\tau) = W(Y,\tau)$. Then we have the following relationships:

$$
\begin{aligned}
V_x &= W_y \exp[-\delta\tau] \\
V_{xx} &= W_{yy} \exp[-2\delta\tau] \\
V_\tau &= W_\tau - \delta Y W_y
\end{aligned}
$$

Substituting into the differential equation and simplifying, we have:

$$\tfrac{1}{2}\sigma^2 Y^2 W_{yy} + rYW_y - \pi rW - W_\tau = 0$$

This is equivalent to the equation we derived in the previous section. Provided the boundary conditions are unaffected by the change in variables, we can state that the value of a derivative security can be determined from equilibrium considerations. In particular, if the underlying security follows geometric Brownian motion and earns a return that is below equilibrium by an amount $\delta$, we substitute $X\exp[-\delta\tau]$ for X, and value the derivative as if the security earned an equilibrium rate of return.

How can this result be applied? Consider the forward valuation result in the previous section:

$$V = X\exp[r(1 - \pi)\tau]$$

If X earns a rate of return that is below the equilibrium return by an amount $\delta$, the valuation equation becomes:

$$V = X\exp[(r(1 - \pi) - \delta)\tau]$$

If X is a stock index and dividends are paid continuously at the dollar rate of $\delta Xdt$, the expression for V determines the price of a forward contract on the index level. If X is a cash commodity that incurs proportional carrying costs continuously of $\delta Xdt$, the value of the forward contract will be:

$$V = X\exp[(r(1 - \pi) + \delta)\tau]$$

The same can be said if the commodity earns a convenience yield.

The value of an option can be determined in a similar manner. If we define the Black-Scholes European call option pricing function as $C = C(S,\tau;X,r,\sigma)$ in the no-dividend case, then the value of the call option if the stock pays proportional dividends is $C(S\exp[-\delta\tau],\tau;X,r,\sigma)$. If the call option is written against a futures contract instead of a cash commodity, then its value is given by $C(S\exp[-r(1 - \pi)\tau],\tau;X,r,\sigma)$.

## Time–Dependent Boundary Conditions: The American Option

Until this point, we have considered options of the European variety; these options can only be exercised at a preordained time. Options of the American variety may be exercised at any time up until that preordained time. In fact, one may look at an American option as a European option plus the right to exercise the European option early. Merton (1973) demonstrated that if the stock pays no dividends, the value of this American feature is zero for call options. Therefore, we analyze the case where the stock follows geometric Brownian motion and pays dividends at a constant proportional rate of $\delta Xdt$:[2]

$$dX = (\alpha - \delta)Xdt + \sigma XdZ$$

While the option is alive (before it is exercised), it must satisfy the following partial differential equation:

$$\tfrac{1}{2}\sigma^2 X^2 V_{xx} + (r - \delta)XV_x - rV - V_\tau = 0$$

Strictly speaking, the arbitrage approach cannot be employed here, since the price of the stock earns a below-equilibrium rate of return. We switch to an equilibrium framework, and substitute the certainty-equivalent growth rate for the stock, $r - \delta$, for $\alpha$. See McDonald and Siegel (1984).

---

[2]When a stock pays dividends, and the option holder delays exercise by one moment dt, he gives up $\delta Xdt$ in dividends but receives rEdt in interest on his exercise price. If dividends grow large enough (i.e., X grows large enough), it will eventually be worthwhile to exercise the American call option. The option is not exercised immediately when $\delta X$ exceeds rE, because of the time value; the option holder cannot switch back to holding the option after exercising it.

At this point, the derivation is the same as for a European option. However, we now enforce a time-dependent boundary condition. In this case, the condition may be expressed in terms of either a strategy criterion or a value criterion.

The strategy criterion states that the holder of the option chooses an optimal exercise path $Q = Q(\tau)$. When the stock price X reaches the optimal exercise path, the option is exercised, and the proceeds of X - E are realized. The problem may theoretically be solved by valuing the option for an arbitrary exercise path and then finding the path that optimizes value. This is essentially the approach we followed in Chapter 1 to value the perpetual American call option. In that chapter, we benefited from the perpetual nature of the problem; Q was reduced to a constant. In this case, Q is an unknown function of time.

The value criterion states that the value of the call option must never fall below X - E. If it were to fall below X - E, the trader could immediately make a profit by exercising the option. Furthermore, he could purchase an infinite number of options and increase his profit handsomely![3] Since we normally rule out such arbitrage occurrences, the value criterion is logical. But what about optimality? Since the value of the American call is simply X - E for high enough values of X, its derivative, $V_x$, equals one. There must be a smooth transition between not exercising and exercising; therefore $V_x = 1$ is enforced at the boundary.[4] This condition is called the **high contact condition** or the **smooth pasting condition**.

When X < Q, the equation below is satisfied:

$$\tfrac{1}{2}\sigma^2 X^2 V_{xx} + (r - \delta)X V_x - rV - V_\tau = 0$$

---

[3]Infinitely, in fact.

[4]By hypothesis, $V_x$ is everywhere continuous. There may exist solutions for $V_x$ that are discontinuous at the boundary, but if a continuous solution exists, we hypothesize it would be more appropriate.

But when X > Q, the following equation is satisfied:

$$\tfrac{1}{2}\sigma^2 X^2 V_{xx} + (r - \delta)XV_x - rV - V_\tau = rE - \delta X$$

This equation is derived by calculating the left-hand side for V = X − E. Therefore, there is some discontinuity on the left-hand side of the equation at X = Q. By construction, V and $V_x$ are continuous at X = Q. Therefore, $\tfrac{1}{2}\sigma^2 X^2 V_{xx} - V_\tau$ is discontinuous at the boundary.

The solution to this problem is still unknown, although many authors have contributed to the understanding of the problem, studying the nature of the optimal exercise boundary, and deriving integral expressions for the solution to the value of the American option.

Time-dependent boundary conditions also come to play in the valuation of callable bonds and fixed-rate mortgages. Callable bonds are those that may be repurchased by the issuer at a prespecified price. Theoretically, the value of a callable bond may not exceed the call price plus the direct costs of calling. This boundary condition reflects a value criterion for the valuation of callable bonds. Fixed-rate mortgages fall in the same category; they can be repurchased (i.e., prepaid according to a fixed schedule) at the option of the issuer (homeowner).

For most problems with time-dependent boundary conditions, solutions are not available in closed form for asset values. Numerical estimation techniques must be used to determine fair asset values in this context.

## Exercises

3.1    Consider the valuation of a forward contract when the underlying commodity follows geometric Brownian motion. Assume there are no carrying costs, convenience yield, or dividend considerations. Let the rate of return on the cash commodity be $\alpha = r + \beta(\alpha_m - r)$.

a. What is the relationship between the cash price and the expected future cash price?

b. What is the relationship between the forward price and the expected future cash price?

c. The expectations hypothesis posits that the forward price equals the expected future cash price. Under what conditions is the expectations hypothesis correct?

3.2 What are the effects of carrying costs, convenience yields, and dividend considerations on the relationships in 3.1a and 3.1b?

3.3 Suppose that an underlying commodity's price follows an arithmetic Brownian motion process with drift $\alpha$ and volatility $\sigma$.

a. What economic problems are suggested by the specification? In what instances would these economic problems be avoided?

b. What is the value of a forward contract on this commodity, assuming a proportion of the price, $\pi$, is kept in a zero–interest margin account?

3.4 Suppose the value of an index X follows a mean–reverting process:

$$dX = \kappa(\mu - X)dt + \sigma\sqrt{X}dZ$$

a. For what securities might this specification be appropriate?

b. Value a forward contract on the level of X in $\tau$ periods.

c. How does your answer to 3.4b compare to 3.3b? Why?

3.5    Consider the Black–Scholes solution for the value of the European call option. Let S = Stock value, X = Exercise price, C = Call value, P = Put value and B = exp(-rτ) = Bond value (i.e., T–Bill price per $1 face value that matures on the same date as the option).

    a.    Calculate the necessary partial derivatives and verify the partial differential equation.

    b.    Show that $Sn(d_1) - XBn(d_2) = 0$, where the standardized normal density function is given by $n(z) = exp[-\frac{1}{2}z^2]/\sqrt{(2\pi)}$.

    c.    Calculate and sign the derivatives of the call price with respect to X, r, and σ.

    d.    Calculate and interpret the second partial derivative of the call price with respect to the exercise price.

    e.    Derive the PDE for the value of the put option with the same striking price and time to maturity.

    f.    Value the put option. (*HINT: Let $P(S,\tau) = C(S,\tau) + f(S,\tau)$, and revise the boundary conditions accordingly.*)

    g.    Let M represent an index portfolio that follows geometric Brownian motion with drift $\alpha_m$ and volatility $\sigma_m$. The correlation between dZ and $dZ_m$ is ρdt. Calculate the elasticity of S with respect to M, and of C with respect to M.

3.6    A fixed–rate mortgage is initiated with a loan balance of L, a contract rate of ρ, and a term of τ periods. The coupon is paid continuously at the dollar rate of cdt; c is chosen so that the present value of the payments at the contract rate equals the loan balance. The mortgagor has a prepayment option that is subject to a prepayment penalty of k percent of the outstanding balance if prepaid before u periods pass. After that time, there is no prepayment penalty. The short interest rate follows a mean–reverting square–root process.

Let $P = P(r,\tau)$ be a known pricing function for zero coupon bonds (face value \$1) maturing in $\tau$ periods. Let $M = M(r,\tau)$ represent the market value of the mortgage.

   a.    What partial differential equation must the mortgage price satisfy? *(HINT: Construct a hedge portfolio with a sufficiently long–term discount bond.)*

   b.    What boundary conditions must the mortgage value satisfy?

3.7    Value a European call option on an underlying index, X, that follows arithmetic Brownian motion with drift $\alpha$ and volatility $\sigma$. Use an equilibrium pricing framework in a risk-neutral economy.

   a.    Why is arbitrage pricing implausible?

   b.    What PDE must be satisfied? What boundary conditions?

   c.    What is the value of the call option?

   d.    Verify that the PDE and boundary conditions are satisfied by your solution.

3.8    (Advanced) Value a European option on an underlying index, X, that follows a mean–reverting square root process:

$$dX = (\alpha - \kappa X)\, dt + \sigma\sqrt{X}\, dZ$$

Assume the exercise price is E and that the value of a risk-free zero coupon bond maturing in $\tau$ periods is $B(\tau)$ per \$1 face value. Assume the economy is risk-neutral. Let:

$$\gamma = \sqrt{(\kappa^2 + 2\sigma^2)}$$

$$f(\tau) = [2(e^{\gamma\tau} - 1)]/[\tau((\gamma + \kappa)(e^{\gamma\tau} - 1) + 2\gamma)]$$

$$\xi(\tau) = [\gamma\tau f(\tau)(e^{\gamma\tau} - 1)^{-1}e^{\gamma\tau/2}]^2$$

$$\phi(\tau) \;=\; 4E/[\sigma^2\tau f(\tau)]$$

$$\psi(\tau) \;=\; \alpha\tau f(\tau)Q(\phi,\upsilon + 2,\eta)$$

where $Q(\phi,\upsilon,\eta) = 1 - \chi^2(\phi,\upsilon,\eta)$, the complementary noncentral Chi-squared distribution function with $\upsilon$ degrees of freedom and noncentrality parameter $\eta$. *(HINT: If you can't derive this, you may wish to check that the solution verifies the PDE you derived.)*

## Solutions to Exercises

3.1    a.    $E(C_t) = C_0\exp(\alpha t)$

        b.    $F_0 = E(C_t)\exp[(r - \alpha)t]$

        c.    $r = \alpha$ or $\beta = 0$

3.2    a.    $E(C_t) = C_0\exp[(r + c - d - y)t]$; $r$ = risk-free rate, $c$ = carrying costs, $d$ = dividend yield, $y$ = convenience yield. All variables represent proportional costs or benefits incurred continuously.

        b.    See 3.1b., but $\alpha = \alpha' + c - d - y$, where $\alpha'$ is the net capital appreciation rate.

3.3    a.    The assumption admits the possibility of negative prices in the future and exhibits nonconstant proportional growth. The problem could be avoided by explicitly accounting for cessation of the process when it reaches an absorbing barrier.

        b.    $V = X\exp[r(1 - \pi)\tau]$

3.4    a.    It would be difficult to assume that security values could satisfy this process. However, if the forward contract is based on an interest rate index, the comparison is feasible. However, the tradability of the underlying asset is in question.

        b.    $V = X\exp[r(1 - \pi)\tau]$

c.  The answers are the same because the analysis assumes the underlying security is tradable, and the drift (however economically inappropriate) is included in the price of the traded security. The volatility doesn't matter because of the equivalence of the risk-neutral pricing result in this arbitrage framework.

3.5  a.  $C_s = N(d_1)$, $C_{ss} = n(d_1)/[S\sigma\sqrt{\tau}]$,
$C_\tau = \frac{1}{2}\sigma XBn(d_2)/\sqrt{\tau} + rXBN(d_2)$

Note that

$C_s = SN'(d_1)/(S\sigma\sqrt{\tau}) - XN'(d_2)/(S\sigma\sqrt{\tau}) + N(d_1)$

b.  Left to reader.

c.  $C_x = -BN(d_2) < 0$; $C_r = \tau XBN(d_2) > 0$; $C_\sigma = \sqrt{\tau}XBn(d_2) > 0$

d.  $C_{xx} = B[n(d_2)/(X\sigma\sqrt{\tau})]$; the term in brackets is the risk-neutral lognormal density function for S in $\tau$ periods, evaluated at $S = X$.

e.  Same PDE; b.c. (boundary condition) differs

f.  $f(S,\tau) = XB - S$

g.  $\beta_s = \rho_{sm}\sigma_s/\sigma_m$; $\beta_c = \beta_s N(d_1)S/C$

3.6  a.  $c = \rho L/[1 - \exp(-\rho\tau)]$; $h = -M_r/P_r$
$r(M + hP) = \frac{1}{2}(M_{rr} + hP_{rr})\sigma^2 r - (M_\tau + hP_\tau) + c$

b.  $M \le (1 + kI)c[1 - \exp(-\rho\tau)]/\rho$ for all $\tau$; $I = 1$ if $t \le u$ and 0 otherwise. $M(r,0) = 0$.

3.7  a.  A process that follows arithmetic Brownian motion cannot represent a security price; for example, X may become negative. Also, a linear average growth rate seems to invite arbitrage.

b.  $\frac{1}{2}\sigma^2 C_{XX} + \alpha C_X - rC - C_\tau = 0$;
$C(X,0) = \text{Max}(X - E,0)$

c.    $d = (X + \alpha\tau - E)/(\sigma\sqrt{\tau})$;

   $C = \sigma\sqrt{\tau}(e^{-r\tau})[dN(d) + n(d)$

   $N(z)$ is the cumulative standard normal distribution function, and $n(z)$ is the standard normal frequency.

d.    Left to reader.

3.8    The solution is adapted from Longstaff, "The Valuation of Options on Yields," 1990.

$C = B(\tau)[XQ(\phi,\upsilon + 4,\eta)\xi - EQ(\phi,\upsilon,\eta) + \psi]$

# 4

# Optimal Decision Strategies and Valuation

## Introduction

In many cases, the value of an asset depends on the way the asset is managed. Assuming the asset is managed optimally, in a risk-neutral economy, the value of the asset will be found by discounting cash flows at the risk-free rate. In a risk-averse economy under some conditions, the growth rate can be altered until risk-neutral discounting is feasible.

All problems in the chapter deal with the basic logic of maximizing the present value of future receipts. Use the risk-free rate if the state variable drifts are transposed to their certainty-equivalent growth rates. The nature of the maximization may differ from one problem to the next, as will boundary conditions.

This chapter discusses a class of optimization problems and provides the intutive motivation behind the methods used to solve these problems. These methods have been used by many authors to study equilibrium, strategy, and valuation in financial settings. The first part of the chapter presents the simplest case, an infinite horizon problem. If the optimal control for a problem in this class is constant, one can use the principle of the maximum or ordinary calculus techniques to learn the value of the asset. One such example is constructed here. The chapter then expands the analysis to similar problems with multiple state variables and explicit time-dependence. Lastly, the chapter presents one of Merton's classic results in financial economics. The optimal consumption and portfolio rules of Merton are derived using these techniques.

## A Time–Homogeneous Financial Maximization Problem

This section begins with the analysis of an infinite horizon problem. The advantage of these **time–homogeneous** problems is that the value of the asset does not depend explicitly upon time. This eliminates one variable from the partial differential equation derived. If the optimization is taken over a finite period of time, the problem is termed **time–inhomogeneous**.

The general problem can be stated in a more comprehensive manner; our approach here is to diagram the solution of a problem typical of financial applications. The interested reader may pursue more advanced techniques such as those in Malliaris and Brock (1986).

We wish to maximize the value of an asset, V, which depends on some set of state variables, X, a time variable, t, and parameters of the problem. In addition, the value of V may be influenced by some control, $\xi$. For a univariate stochastic process X, the problem may be written:

$$V = \max_{\xi} E_0 \int_0^{\infty} e^{-rs} u(X,\xi) ds$$

$$\text{s.t. } dX = \alpha(X,\xi) ds + \sigma(X,\xi) dW$$

Of particular interest is the infinite horizon of this problem together with the independence of u, $\alpha$, and $\sigma$ from s, an index for calendar time. We will generalize this analysis somewhat later in the chapter.

In some cases, $\xi$ will be a constant. If a closed-form solution can be determined for V, then $\xi$ may be chosen by ordinary calculus techniques to maximize the value of V. One may also employ the stochastic principle of the maximum, which permits the study of more complex controls.

We motivate the discussion of the stochastic principle of the maximum with financial intuition. In a risk–neutral world, how does one find the value of an asset whose value may be influenced by a particular management strategy? First, one finds the optimal management strategy for the asset. Under this optimal strategy, the expected cash flows are computed and discounted at the risk-free rate. In other words, the total return of the optimally managed asset must equal the risk-free rate. If the risk in the relevant state variables is priced risk, the growth rates must be altered to their certainty–equivalents before this calculation can be made.

For the time being, think of $u(X,\xi)$ as a cash flow and of r as the discount factor. The expected cash flows from V (at every moment s) are:

$$ECF = u(X,\xi)ds$$

The expected capital appreciation on V comes from Itô's lemma:

$$CG = dV = (V_x dX + \tfrac{1}{2}V_{xx}dX^2)$$

$$ECG = [V_x \alpha(X,\xi) + \tfrac{1}{2}V_{xx}\sigma^2(X,\xi)]\, dt$$

Note that the value of V does not depend on time. The optimally managed total return per unit time is given by:

$$\begin{aligned} ETR &= \max[ECF + ECG] \\ &= \max_\xi [u(X,\xi) + V_x \alpha(X,\xi) + \tfrac{1}{2}V_{xx}\sigma^2(X,\xi)] \end{aligned}$$

From our earlier discussion, the total expected return per unit time must be equivalent to the riskless return in a risk–neutral economy. Therefore:

$$rV = \max_\xi [u(X,\xi) + V_x \alpha(X,\xi) + \tfrac{1}{2}V_{xx}\sigma^2(X,\xi)]$$

To maximize the expression in brackets, one may use ordinary calculus if $\xi$ is constant, constrained maximization methods if $\xi$ is variable and constrained, or the calculus of variations. In any of these methods, one treats V, $V_x$, and $V_{xx}$ as constants.

Once the maximizing $\xi$ is found, the differential equation may be solved using the techniques presented in Chapter 2. Unfortunately, the solution will rarely satisfy one of the four basic valuation cases. In this text, we defer the reader to more advanced texts to learn how to solve the usually nonlinear differential equations we will encounter in this section.

We will now demonstrate a technique whereby the stochastic principle of the maximum may be employed. The following simple example can be solved using either method.

## Example Using the Principle of the Maximum

Suppose X follows arithmetic Brownian motion, with drift $\alpha$ and volatility $\sigma$. An asset pays continuous cash flows forever at a rate of Xdt. Cash flows may become negative; in this case, the firm is responsible for raising equity to meet the cash requirements. There is no limited liability option. A manager may influence the growth rate of X, albeit at a cost. Suppose that for a given choice of $\alpha$, the shareholders would have to pay $\alpha^2 dt$ continuously to managers. Therefore, higher effort ($\alpha$) increases not only the growth rate of cash flows but also the management cost. We assume $\alpha > 0$. Then, we wish to find V, the value of the cash flows net of management expenses:

$$V = \max_\alpha E_0 \int_0^\infty e^{-rs}(X - \alpha^2)ds$$

$$\text{s.t. } dX = \alpha ds + \sigma dZ$$

Using the principle of the maximum, we have:

$$ECF = (X - \alpha^2)\, dt$$

$$CG = dV = V_x dX + \tfrac{1}{2}V_{xx}(dX)^2$$

$$\text{ECG} = [\alpha V_x + \tfrac{1}{2}\sigma^2 V_{xx}] \, dt$$

$$\text{ETR} = \max_\alpha [\text{ECF} + \text{ECG}]$$

$$rV = \max_\alpha [X - \alpha^2 + \alpha V_x + \tfrac{1}{2}\sigma^2 V_{xx}]$$

Taking the ordinary derivative of the expression in brackets, we learn:

$$-2\alpha^* + V_x = 0 \Rightarrow V_x = 2\alpha^*$$

The second derivative is unconditionally negative, suggesting an interior local maximum has been found. We assume $\alpha^*$ is constant; therefore $V_{xx} = 0$, and $V = 2X\alpha^* + C$, where C is an undetermined constant. Substituting into the differential equation, we have:

$$rV = r[2X\alpha^* + C] = [X - \alpha^{*2} + 2\alpha^{*2}] = X + \alpha^* 2$$

Since the differential equation holds true for all values of X, the coefficients of X must match as well as the constants:

$$2\alpha^* r = 1 \Rightarrow \alpha^* = 1/(2r)$$

$$rC = \alpha^* 2 \Rightarrow C = 1/(4r^3)$$

Therefore, $V = X/r + 1/(4r^3)$.

## An Alternative Substitution
In the previous section, we solved for V and its derivatives in terms of $\alpha^*$. It is also possible to substitute for $\alpha$ the optimal functions of V and its derivatives in the PDE In this case, the PDE becomes:

$$rV = X - (V_x/2)^2 + (V_x/2)V_x + \frac{1}{2}\sigma^2 V_{xx}$$

$$rV = X + (V_x/2)^2 + \frac{1}{2}\sigma^2 V_{xx}$$

This PDE may be solved for the asset value as well. To verify the PDE, we substitute from our solution for V above:

$$r[X/r + 1/(4r^3)] = X + [1/(2r)]^2 + 0$$

which checks easily.

## Same Example Using Ordinary Calculus

We use the methodology of Chapter 1 to obtain the value of a linearly growing perpetuity (arithmetic Brownian motion) minus a level perpetuity of $\alpha^2$:

$$V = X/r + \alpha/r^2 - \alpha^2/r$$

This result may be verified by discounting expected cash flows over an infinite horizon. The first two terms correspond to the value of a linearly growing perpetuity in continuous time, and the third term corresponds to the cost of maintaining that growth. The analysis assumes $\alpha$ is an unknown constant.

Differentiate with respect to $\alpha$ and set $V_\alpha = 0$:

$$V_\alpha = 0 = 1/r^2 - 2\alpha/r$$

which implies that:

$$\alpha^* = 1/2r$$

Substituting into the expression for V, we have:

$$V = X/r + 1/(4r^3)$$

# Extensions of the Basic Methodology

## Extension to Multiple State Variables

If there is more than one stochastic variable (but value does not depend on time) in the problem, the extension is straightforward. Using the multivariate extension of Itô's Lemma presented in Chapter 1, we can calculate dV and E[dV] in a straightforward manner. The partial differential equation derived, of course, retains the extra state variable.

## Example

Consider a perpetually lived value-maximizing monopolist who produces output at a rate of qdt, but faces a stochastically varying demand curve. In particular, the demand curve is linear and of the form $p = a - bq$, where p is the price of the good, and a and b follow the stochastic system:

$$da = f(a,b,q)dt + \sigma(a,b,q)dZ_a$$

$$db = g(a,b,q)dt + v(a,b,q)dZ_b$$

$$dZ_a dZ_b = \rho dt$$

subject to the initial conditions $a(0) = a_0$ and $b(0) = b_0$. The cost of production of the good is zero. A financial economist wants to value the firm in a risk-neutral economy; therefore, he assumes the value of the firm, V, satisfies:

$$V = \max_q E_0 \int_0^\infty e^{-rs}(a - bq)q \ ds$$

To find the optimal management strategy, we note that the expected "cash flow" component is:

$$ECF = (a - bq)q \, dt$$

that the capital gain component is:

$$dV = V_a da + V_b db + \tfrac{1}{2} V_{aa} da^2 + V_{ab} da db + \tfrac{1}{2} V_{bb} db^2$$

and that the expected capital gain component is:

$$ECG = E[dV] = V_a f + V_b g + \tfrac{1}{2} V_{aa} \sigma^2 + V_{ab} \sigma v \rho + \tfrac{1}{2} V_{bb} v^2$$

Because of our assumption of a risk-neutral economy, the maximum total return is given by:

$$\max(TR) = \max(ECF + ECG) = rV$$

Therefore, the following PDE must be satisfied:

$$rV = \max_q \left[ (a - bq)q + V_a f + V_b g + \tfrac{1}{2} V_{aa} \sigma^2 + V_{ab} \sigma v \rho + \tfrac{1}{2} V_{bb} v^2 \right]$$

The first order condition for an interior maximum is:

$$a - 2bq + V_a f_q + V_b g_q + V_{aa} \sigma \sigma_q + V_{ab} \rho [\sigma v_q + \sigma_q v] + V_{bb} v v_q = 0$$

We may now analyze some special cases of this problem.

### Example Case A: No Intertemporal Strategic Motives

If $f(\cdot) = a f_0$, $g(\cdot) = b g_0$, $\sigma(\cdot) = a \sigma_0$, and $v(\cdot) = b v_0$ where $f_0$, $g_0$, $\sigma_0$, and $v_0$ are constants, then $q = \tfrac{1}{2} a/b$, the same solution as the single-period case. The PDE reduces to:

$$rV = a^2/(4b) + V_a a f_0 + V_b b g_0 + \tfrac{1}{2} V_{aa} a^2 \sigma_0^2 + V_{ab} a b \sigma_0 v_0 \rho + \tfrac{1}{2} V_{bb} b^2 v_0^2$$

If $V = V(a,b)$, then the solution satisfies the boundary conditions $V(0,b) = 0$, $V(a,0) = \infty$, $V(a,\infty) = 0$, and $V(\infty,b) = \infty$. The value of the firm is given by $V = a^2/[4b(r - k)]$ where $k = 2f_0 - g_0 + \tfrac{1}{2}\sigma_0^2 - 2\rho\sigma_0 v_0 + v_0^2$.

## Example Case B: Intertemporal Strategic Motives

Suppose that the monopolist's good can be stored through time, so that production in every instant affects future sales prices. In particular we assume that $f(a,b,q) = (f_0 - cq)a$, where c is a positive constant. We assume the other terms are as defined in example case A. In case B, the higher the production rate climbs, the lower will fall the expected future price of the good.

The first order (interior) condition for value maximization is:

$$q = a(1 - cV_a)/(2b)$$

Substituting into the PDE we learn:

$$rV = \frac{a^2}{4b} + V_a a\left(f - \frac{ac}{2b}\right) + V_a^2 a^2\left(\frac{c^2}{4b}\right)$$

$$+ V_b bg + \tfrac{1}{2}V_{aa}a^2\sigma^2 + V_{ab}ab\rho\sigma v + \tfrac{1}{2}V_{bb}b^2v^2$$

The differential equation can be reduced to dependence upon a single variable by making the substitution $V(a,b;c) = W(a;d)/b$ where $d = c/(2b)$. Under this substitution, the PDE becomes:

$$rW = \frac{a^2}{4} + W_a(af - a^2d - g - a\rho\sigma v + v^2) + \tfrac{1}{2}a^2W_{aa}\sigma^2 + W_a^2a^2d^2$$

## Extension to Explicit Time Dependence

In theory, the extension of the basic model to incorporate explicit time dependence is straightforward. However, the computational difficulty is often magnified by this seemingly simple extension. We consider once again the maximization problem, but add a few features:

$$V = \max_\xi E_0\left(\int_0^\tau e^{-rs} u(X,s,\xi)\, ds + e^{-r\tau}B(X(\tau),\tau)\right)$$

$$\text{s.t. } dX = \alpha(X,t,\xi)dt + \sigma(X,t,\xi)dZ$$

Notably, the optimization is taken over a fixed time horizon, and a final "bequest" function is included in the objective function. Of course, depending on the problem, the interpretation of the bequest function will differ. For example, a manager may wish to maximize the dollar value of his utility plus share holdings at a fixed termination date in the future. If the maturity date is random, and if the maturity is determined according to a Poisson arrival process, the extension is straightforward.

Following our earlier methodology, we note the expected "cash flows," "capital gains," and "total returns" are:

$$\begin{aligned}
\text{ECF} &= u(X,\xi,s) \\
\text{ECG} &= E(dV) = V_x\alpha + \tfrac{1}{2}V_{xx}\sigma^2 - V_\tau \\
\text{ETR} &= \max [\text{ECF} + \text{ECG}] = rVdt
\end{aligned}$$

Notice that the use of Itô's Lemma to calculate expected capital gains now contains the time derivative. Combined together, this gives us a differential equation similar to the one derived in the first section:

$$rV + V_\tau = \max_\xi [u(X,\xi,\tau) + V_x\alpha(X,\xi,\tau) + \tfrac{1}{2}V_{xx}\sigma^2(X,\xi,\tau)]$$

The difference is in the left side of the equation, which includes the time derivative. Also, additional boundary conditions must be satisfied. Consider the behavior of V as $\tau \to 0$:

$$V(X,0) = B(X,0)$$

The resulting PDE may be solved by many methods, including the educated guess method, the Laplace transform method, or the Fourier transform method. In the likely absence of a closed-form solution, numerical approximation methods may be used.

## A Classic Problem in Financial Economics

The following section is adapted from Merton (1971). We consider an application of the Markowitz theory of portfolio selection to securities in a continuous-time economy. We examine the case of a single risky asset and a risk-free security in a one–period discrete-time model. Consider the problem of choosing portfolio weights to maximize expected utility:

$$U = r - \tfrac{1}{2}A\sigma^2$$

which is quadratic in the variance of a risky asset ($\sigma^2$). The expected return on the risky asset is r, and the risk-free rate is $r_f$. The individual's coefficient of risk aversion is A. If $\omega$ is the proportion invested in the risky asset, then for an arbitrary portfolio composed of the two assets we have:

$$r_p = \omega r + (1 - \omega)r_f$$

$$\sigma_p^2 = \omega^2\sigma^2$$

Maximizing expected utility over choices of W, we find that:

$$w = (r - r_f)/(A\sigma^2)$$

If the assets trade in continuous time, the optimal portfolio holdings are similar if the investment opportunity set is constant. We define **investment opportunity set** as the set of expected returns, variances and correlations between securities. We can formulate the problem as follows:

An individual wishes to make portfolio decisions that maximize his discounted lifetime utility of consumption (c); his utility at every instant is $U(c) = c^\gamma/\gamma$, and his continuous discount rate is $\rho$.

His initial wealth is W, which can be divided at all times between two assets. The first asset has value X, which follows geometric Brownian motion, with drift $\alpha$ and volatility $\sigma$. The second asset (P) is risk-free and earns the risk-free rate continuously:

$$dX = \alpha X\ dt + \sigma X\ dZ$$
$$dP = rP\ dt$$

Markets are perfect; there are no taxes, transaction costs, trading restrictions, or other impediments to free, symmetric, and costless trade. Let $\omega$ represent the proportion of wealth invested in the risky asset. Normalize X and P to a current value of 1.

**The Budget Equation.**    The consumer's change in wealth each period comes from investment proceeds minus consumption:

$$dW = [\omega W \alpha X + (1 - \omega)WrP - c]\ dt + \omega W \sigma X\ dZ$$

**The Objective Function.**    The consumer seeks to maximize expected lifetime discounted utility:

$$J = \max_{(c,\omega)} E_0 \int_0^\infty e^{-\rho s}\ c(s)^\gamma/\gamma\ ds$$

s.t. $dW = [\omega W \alpha X + (1 - \omega)WrP - c]\ dt + \omega W \sigma X\ dZ$

**The Partial Differential Equation.**    This looks like the present value of a cash flow, taken at the continuously compounded rate of $\rho$. This is a time-homogeneous problem (infinite horizon), so the value does not depend on time, and the derivative $J_\tau$ vanishes. Then we have:

$$ECF = c^\gamma/\gamma\ dt$$

$$\text{CG} = J_W \, dW + \tfrac{1}{2}J_{WW} \, dW^2$$

$$\text{ECG} = [J_W\{\omega W\alpha X + (1 - \omega)WrP - c\} + \tfrac{1}{2}J_{WW}\omega^2 W^2\sigma^2 X^2]dt$$

$$\text{TR} = \rho J = \max_{\{\omega,c\}} [\text{ECF} + \text{ECG}]$$

$$\rho J = \max_{\{\omega,c\}} [c^\gamma/\gamma + J_W\{\omega W\alpha X + (1 - \omega)WrP - c\}$$
$$+ \tfrac{1}{2}J_{WW}\omega^2 W^2\sigma^2 X]$$

**The Optimal Controls.** Treating everything inside the brackets as constants except $\omega$ and $c$, we calculate derivatives to find first order conditions for an interior maximum:

$$c^{\gamma-1} = J_W$$

$$\omega = -J_W(\alpha - r)/[J_{WW}W\sigma^2]$$

$J$ is known as the derived utility of wealth, and $A = -WJ_{WW}/J_W$ is the Arrow–Pratt measure of relative risk aversion. Therefore, $\omega = (\alpha - r)/[A\sigma^2]$, as in the single period case.

**Extensions.** See Merton (1971) for extensions of this methodology along many interesting dimensions.

## Exercises

4.1 Assume that a firm receives net cash flows Xdt generated by an arbitrary Wiener process (before managerial compensation has been deducted). The manager of the firm has some univariate control, $\xi$, over the average growth rate of the cash flows. The drift $\alpha = \alpha(X,\xi)$ is an increasing concave function of $\xi$. The volatility $\sigma = \sigma(X)$ does not depend on managerial effort. We assume the manager puts forth effort that increases in her compensation; to induce effort level $\xi$, the manager must be compensated $C(\xi)$, an increasing convex function. The firm and manager are perpetually lived.

    a.    What is the objective function of the owners of the firm?

    b.    What is the first order condition for optimization of this objective?

    c.    What ODE must the firm value satisfy?

        1.    Express the ODE in terms of the value function.

        2.    Express the ODE in terms of the effort function.

**4.2**    An individual experiences occasional auto accidents, the timing of which are determined by a Poisson arrival process with intensity $\lambda$ chosen by the individual. When an accident occurs, the cost of the accident is given by the contemporaneous level of the process X, which follows geometric Brownian motion with drift $\alpha$ and volatility $\sigma$. The cost to the individual (in terms of lost time and other factors) of maintaining an average accident rate of $\lambda$ dt is $C(\lambda)$ dt, a decreasing convex function of $\lambda$. Of course, $\lambda$ may be chosen optimally through time by the insured.

    a.    If the individual is risk–neutral, what is his objective function?

    b.    Let V represent the expected present value of all future losses due to automobile accidents, net of the cost of maintaining a safe-driving policy. What PDE does V satisfy?

    c.    What is the optimal operating policy for the individual?

    d.    Will the individual's behavior change if he has a perpetual insurance policy that pays a fraction $(1 - \pi)$ of the losses? Assume the cost of the policy is sunk, and the policy life is perpetual.

**4.3**    This is a classic problem in stochastic capital theory. Suppose the height of a tree at time t is represented by $X_t$, which follows arithmetic Brownian motion. We must decide when to cut down the tree to maximize its value. If the tree is worth $1 per unit height, and if the tree is cut down at time $\tau$ at height Y, then the value today is:

$$V = e^{-r\tau}Y.$$

a.   What PDE must the value of the tree satisfy?

b.   What are the relevant boundary conditions?

c.   Value the tree, assuming that the value is zero when the tree's height approaches $-\infty$.

d.   Assume it is optimal to cut down the tree when it reaches a fixed value Y. What is the optimal cutting policy?

4.4   Consider once again the problem of managerial compensation discussed earlier in the chapter. Net revenues were calculated to be $(X - \alpha^2)$, the difference between gross revenues and management costs.

Suppose the government taxes earnings at a constant rate of $\theta$.

a.   Solve for the optimal management strategy and value of the firm assuming that managers are paid from after-tax income. How does the optimal effort level change?

b.   Now assume that management costs can be deducted from income before tax. How does the optimal effort level change?

## Solutions to Exercises

4.1   a.

$$V = \max E \int_{0}^{\infty} e^{-rs}[X - C(\xi)]\,ds$$

s.t. $dX = \alpha(X,\xi)dt + \sigma(X)dZ.$

b. (′ denotes derivative with respect to $\xi$)
$C' = V_x\, \alpha'$

c1. $rV = X - C(\xi^*) + V_x\alpha(X,\xi^*) + \frac{1}{2}V_{xx}\sigma^2(X)$

c2. Replace V with $\int^x (C'/\alpha')dX$, $V_x = C'/\alpha'$,
$V_{xx} = -C'\alpha''/\alpha'^2$

**4.2** a.

$$V = \min E \int_0^\infty e^{-rs}[\lambda X + C(\lambda)]\,ds$$

b. $rV = \max_\lambda\,[\lambda X + C(\lambda) + V_x\alpha X + \frac{1}{2}V_{xx}\sigma^2 X^2]$

c. $X + C'(\lambda) = 0$; as potential accident losses increase, expend effort to reduce $\lambda$.

d. $\pi X + C'(\lambda) = 0$; proportional coinsurance induces less effort on the part of the insured.

**4.3** a. Objective: $V = \text{Max}_\tau\, E_0[\int_0^\infty 0\, ds + e^{-r\tau}X_\tau]$
s.t. $dX = \alpha\, dt + \sigma\, dZ$

ECF $= 0\, dt$

$CG = V_x dX + \frac{1}{2}V_{xx}dX^2$ *(Not time because stopping is triggered by tree height)*

$ECG = [\alpha V_x + \frac{1}{2}\sigma^2 V_{xx}]\, dt$

$TR = \max\,[ECG + ECF] = ECG + ECF$

$rV = \alpha V_x + \frac{1}{2}\sigma^2 V_{xx}$

b. $V(Y)=Y$, $V'(Y) = 0$, $V(-\infty) = 0$

c. $V = Y\exp[\lambda(X - Y)]$; $\lambda = [-\alpha + \sqrt{(\alpha^2 + 2r\sigma^2)}]/\sigma^2$

d. $Y^* = 1/\lambda$.

**4.4** a. Less effort will be exerted. (Details left to reader.)

b. The same effort will be exerted.

# Appendix

## Laplace Transforms[1]

### 29.1. Definition of the Laplace Transform

#### One-dimensional Laplace Transform

$$29.1.1 \qquad f(s) = \mathscr{L}\{F(t)\} = \int_0^\infty e^{-st} F(t)dt$$

$F(t)$ is a function of the real variable $t$ and $s$ is a complex variable. $F(t)$ is called the original function and $f(s)$ is called the image function. If the integral in 29.1.1 converges for a real $s=s_0$, i.e.,

$$\lim_{\substack{A\to 0 \\ B\to\infty}} \int_A^B e^{-s_0 t} F(t)dt$$

exists, then it converges for all $s$ with $\mathscr{R}s > s_0$, and the image function is a single valued analytic function of $s$ in the half-plane $\mathscr{R}s > s_0$.

#### Two-dimensional Laplace Transform

$$29.1.2 \qquad f(u,v) = \mathscr{L}\{F(x,y)\} = \int_0^\infty \int_0^\infty e^{-ux-vy} F(x,y)dxdy$$

#### Definition of the Unit Step Function

$$29.1.3 \qquad u(t) = \begin{cases} 0 & (t<0) \\ \tfrac{1}{2} & (t=0) \\ 1 & (t>0) \end{cases}$$

In the following tables the factor $u(t)$ is to be understood as multiplying the original function $F(t)$.

### 29.2. Operations for the Laplace Transform[1]

| | Original Function $F(t)$ | Image Function $f(s)$ |
|---|---|---|
| 29.2.1 | $F(t)$ | $\int_0^\infty e^{-st} F(t)dt$ |
| | **Inversion Formula** | |
| 29.2.2 | $\dfrac{1}{2\pi i}\int_{c-i\infty}^{c+i\infty} e^{ts} f(s)ds$ | $f(s)$ |
| | **Linearity Property** | |
| 29.2.3 | $AF(t)+BG(t)$ | $Af(s)+Bg(s)$ |
| | **Differentiation** | |
| 29.2.4 | $F'(t)$ | $sf(s)-F(+0)$ |
| 29.2.5 | $F^{(n)}(t)$ | $s^n f(s)-s^{n-1}F(+0)-s^{n-2}F'(+0)-\ldots-F^{(n-1)}(+0)$ |
| | **Integration** | |
| 29.2.6 | $\int_0^t F(\tau)d\tau$ | $\dfrac{1}{s}f(s)$ |
| 29.2.7 | $\int_0^t \int_0^\tau F(\lambda)d\lambda d\tau$ | $\dfrac{1}{s^2}f(s)$ |
| | **Convolution (Faltung) Theorem** | |
| 29.2.8 | $\int_0^t F_1(t-\tau)F_2(\tau)d\tau = F_1 * F_2$ | $f_1(s)f_2(s)$ |
| | | **Differentiation** |
| 29.2.9 | $-tF(t)$ | $f'(s)$ |
| 29.2.10 | $(-1)^n t^n F(t)$ | $f^{(n)}(s)$ |

---

[1]Reprinted from Chapter 29 of *Handbook of Mathematical Functions* edited by Milton Abramowitz and Irene A. Stegun, (New York: Dover Publications, Inc., 1965).

|  | *Original Function $F(t)$* | *Image Function $f(s)$* |
|---|---|---|

**29.2.11** $\quad\dfrac{1}{t}F(t)$

Integration
$$\int_s^\infty f(x)dx$$

**29.2.12** $\quad e^{at}F(t)$

Linear Transformation
$$f(s-a)$$

**29.2.13** $\quad\dfrac{1}{c}F\left(\dfrac{t}{c}\right)\quad (c>0)$
$$f(cs)$$

**29.2.14** $\quad\dfrac{1}{c}e^{(b/c)t}F\left(\dfrac{t}{c}\right)\quad (c>0)$
$$f(cs-b)$$

**Translation**

**29.2.15** $\quad F(t-b)u(t-b)\quad (b>0)$
$$e^{-bs}f(s)$$

**Periodic Functions**

**29.2.16** $\quad F(t+a)=F(t)$
$$\frac{\int_0^a e^{-st}F(t)dt}{1-e^{-as}}$$

**29.2.17** $\quad F(t+a)=-F(t)$
$$\frac{\int_0^a e^{-st}F(t)dt}{1+e^{-as}}$$

**Half-Wave Rectification of $F(t)$ in 29.2.17**

**29.2.18** $\quad F(t)\displaystyle\sum_{n=0}^\infty (-1)^n u(t-na)$
$$\frac{f(s)}{1-e^{-as}}$$

**Full-Wave Rectification of $F(t)$ in 29.2.17**

**29.2.19** $\quad |F(t)|$
$$f(s)\coth\frac{as}{2}$$

**Heaviside Expansion Theorem**

**29.2.20** $\quad\displaystyle\sum_{n=1}^m \frac{p(a_n)}{q'(a_n)}e^{a_n t}$
$$\frac{p(s)}{q(s)},\ q(s)=(s-a_1)(s-a_2)\ldots(s-a_m)$$
$$p(s)\ \text{a polynomial of degree}<m$$

**29.2.21** $\quad e^{at}\displaystyle\sum_{n=1}^r \frac{p^{(r-n)}(a)}{(r-n)!}\frac{t^{n-1}}{(n-1)!}$
$$\frac{p(s)}{(s-a)^r}$$
$$p(s)\ \text{a polynomial of degree}<r$$

### 29.3. Table of Laplace Transforms[2,3]

For a comprehensive table of Laplace and other integral transforms see [29.9]. For a table of two-dimensional Laplace transforms see [29.11].

|  | $f(s)$ | $F(t)$ |
|---|---|---|
| **29.3.1** | $\dfrac{1}{s}$ | $1$ |
| **29.3.2** | $\dfrac{1}{s^2}$ | $t$ |

---

[2] The numbers in bold type in the $f(s)$ and $F(t)$ columns indicate the chapters in which the properties of the respective higher mathematical functions are given.

[3] Adapted by permission from R. V. Churchill, Operational mathematics, 2d. ed., McGraw-Hill Book Co., Inc., New York, N. Y., 1958.

|  | $f(s)$ | $F(t)$ |
|---|---|---|
| **29.3.3** | $\dfrac{1}{s^n}$  $(n=1,2,3,\ldots)$ | $\dfrac{t^{n-1}}{(n-1)!}$ |
| **29.3.4** | $\dfrac{1}{\sqrt{s}}$ | $\dfrac{1}{\sqrt{\pi t}}$ |
| **29.3.5** | $s^{-3/2}$ | $2\sqrt{t/\pi}$ |
| **29.3.6** | $s^{-(n+\frac{1}{2})}$  $(n=1,2,3,\ldots)$ | $\dfrac{2^n t^{n-\frac{1}{2}}}{1\cdot 3\cdot 5\ldots(2n-1)\sqrt{\pi}}$ |
| **29.3.7** | $\dfrac{\Gamma(k)}{s^k}$  $(k>0)$ | $t^{k-1}$ |
| **29.3.8** | $\dfrac{1}{s+a}$ | $e^{-at}$ |
| **29.3.9** | $\dfrac{1}{(s+a)^2}$ | $te^{-at}$ |
| **29.3.10** | $\dfrac{1}{(s+a)^n}$  $(n=1,2,3,\ldots)$ | $\dfrac{t^{n-1}e^{-at}}{(n-1)!}$ |
| **29.3.11** | $\dfrac{\Gamma(k)}{(s+a)^k}$  $(k>0)$ | $t^{k-1}e^{-at}$ |
| **29.3.12** | $\dfrac{1}{(s+a)(s+b)}$  $(a\neq b)$ | $\dfrac{e^{-at}-e^{-bt}}{b-a}$ |
| **29.3.13** | $\dfrac{s}{(s+a)(s+b)}$  $(a\neq b)$ | $\dfrac{ae^{-at}-be^{-bt}}{a-b}$ |
| **29.3.14** | $\dfrac{1}{(s+a)(s+b)(s+c)}$ | $-\dfrac{(b-c)e^{-at}+(c-a)e^{-bt}+(a-b)e^{-ct}}{(a-b)(b-c)(c-a)}$ |
|  | $(a,b,c \text{ distinct constants})$ | |
| **29.3.15** | $\dfrac{1}{s^2+a^2}$ | $\dfrac{1}{a}\sin at$ |
| **29.3.16** | $\dfrac{s}{s^2+a^2}$ | $\cos at$ |
| **29.3.17** | $\dfrac{1}{s^2-a^2}$ | $\dfrac{1}{a}\sinh at$ |
| **29.3.18** | $\dfrac{s}{s^2-a^2}$ | $\cosh at$ |
| **29.3.19** | $\dfrac{1}{s(s^2+a^2)}$ | $\dfrac{1}{a^2}(1-\cos at)$ |
| **29.3.20** | $\dfrac{1}{s^2(s^2+a^2)}$ | $\dfrac{1}{a^3}(at-\sin at)$ |
| **29.3.21** | $\dfrac{1}{(s^2+a^2)^2}$ | $\dfrac{1}{2a^3}(\sin at-at\cos at)$ |

| | $f(s)$ | $F(t)$ | |
|---|---|---|---|
| **29.3.22** | $\dfrac{s}{(s^2+a^2)^2}$ | $\dfrac{t}{2a}\sin at$ | |
| **29.3.23** | $\dfrac{s^2}{(s^2+a^2)^2}$ | $\dfrac{1}{2a}(\sin at + at\cos at)$ | |
| **29.3.24** | $\dfrac{s^2-a^2}{(s^2+a^2)^2}$ | $t\cos at$ | |
| **29.3.25** | $\dfrac{s}{(s^2+a^2)(s^2+b^2)}\quad (a^2\neq b^2)$ | $\dfrac{\cos at - \cos bt}{b^2-a^2}$ | |
| **29.3.26** | $\dfrac{1}{(s+a)^2+b^2}$ | $\dfrac{1}{b}e^{-at}\sin bt$ | |
| **29.3.27** | $\dfrac{s+a}{(s+a)^2+b^2}$ | $e^{-at}\cos bt$ | |
| **29.3.28** | $\dfrac{3a^2}{s^3+a^3}$ | $e^{-at}-e^{\frac12 at}\left(\cos\dfrac{at\sqrt3}{2}-\sqrt3\sin\dfrac{at\sqrt3}{2}\right)$ | |
| **29.3.29** | $\dfrac{4a^3}{s^4+4a^4}$ | $\sin at\cosh at - \cos at\sinh at$ | |
| **29.3.30** | $\dfrac{s}{s^4+4a^4}$ | $\dfrac{1}{2a^2}\sin at\sinh at$ | |
| **29.3.31** | $\dfrac{1}{s^4-a^4}$ | $\dfrac{1}{2a^3}(\sinh at - \sin at)$ | |
| **29.3.32** | $\dfrac{s}{s^4-a^4}$ | $\dfrac{1}{2a^2}(\cosh at - \cos at)$ | |
| **29.3.33** | $\dfrac{8a^3s^2}{(s^2+a^2)^3}$ | $(1+a^2t^2)\sin at - at\cos at$ | |
| **29.3.34** | $\dfrac{1}{s}\left(\dfrac{s-1}{s}\right)^n$ | $L_n(t)$ | **22** |
| **29.3.35** | $\dfrac{s}{(s+a)^{\frac32}}$ | $\dfrac{1}{\sqrt{\pi t}}e^{-at}(1-2at)$ | |
| **29.3.36** | $\sqrt{s+a}-\sqrt{s+b}$ | $\dfrac{1}{2\sqrt{\pi t^3}}(e^{-bt}-e^{-at})$ | |
| **29.3.37** | $\dfrac{1}{\sqrt{s}+a}$ | $\dfrac{1}{\sqrt{\pi t}}-ae^{a^2t}\,\mathrm{erfc}\,a\sqrt{t}$ | **7** |
| **29.3.38** | $\dfrac{\sqrt{s}}{s-a^2}$ | $\dfrac{1}{\sqrt{\pi t}}+ae^{a^2t}\,\mathrm{erf}\,a\sqrt{t}$ | **7** |
| **29.3.39** | $\dfrac{\sqrt{s}}{s+a^2}$ | $\dfrac{1}{\sqrt{\pi t}}-\dfrac{2a}{\sqrt{\pi}}\,e^{-a^2t}\displaystyle\int_0^{a\sqrt{t}}e^{\lambda^2}d\lambda$ | **7** |
| **29.3.40** | $\dfrac{1}{\sqrt{s}(s-a^2)}$ | $\dfrac{1}{a}e^{a^2t}\,\mathrm{erf}\,a\sqrt{t}$ | **7** |

| | $f(s)$ | | $F(t)$ | |
|---|---|---|---|---|
| **29.3.41** | $\dfrac{1}{\sqrt{s}\,(s+a^2)}$ | | $\dfrac{2}{a\sqrt{\pi}}\,e^{-a^2t}\displaystyle\int_0^{a\sqrt{t}} e^{\lambda^2}d\lambda$ | **7** |
| **29.3.42** | $\dfrac{b^2-a^2}{(s-a^2)(b+\sqrt{s})}$ | | $e^{a^2t}[b-a\ \text{erf}\ a\sqrt{t}]-be^{b^2t}\ \text{erfc}\ b\sqrt{t}$ | **7** |
| **29.3.43** | $\dfrac{1}{\sqrt{s}(\sqrt{s}+a)}$ | | $e^{a^2t}\ \text{erfc}\ a\sqrt{t}$ | **7** |
| **29.3.44** | $\dfrac{1}{(s+a)\sqrt{s+b}}$ | | $\dfrac{1}{\sqrt{b-a}}\,e^{-at}\ \text{erf}\ (\sqrt{b-a}\sqrt{t})$ | **7** |
| **29.3.45** | $\dfrac{b^2-a^2}{\sqrt{s}(s-a^2)(\sqrt{s}+b)}$ | | $e^{a^2t}\left[\dfrac{b}{a}\ \text{erf}\ (a\sqrt{t})-1\right]+e^{b^2t}\ \text{erfc}\ b\sqrt{t}$ | **7** |
| **29.3.46** | $\dfrac{(1-s)^n}{s^{n+\frac12}}$ | | $\dfrac{n!}{(2n)!\sqrt{\pi t}}\,H_{2n}(\sqrt{t})$ | **22** |
| **29.3.47** | $\dfrac{(1-s)^n}{s^{n+\frac32}}$ | | $\dfrac{n!}{(2n+1)!\sqrt{\pi}}\,H_{2n+1}(\sqrt{t})$ | **22** |
| **29.3.48** | $\dfrac{\sqrt{s+2a}}{\sqrt{s}}-1$ | | $ae^{-at}[I_1(at)+I_0(at)]$ | **9** |
| **29.3.49** | $\dfrac{1}{\sqrt{s+a}\sqrt{s+b}}$ | | $e^{-\frac12(a+b)t}I_0\left(\dfrac{a-b}{2}\,t\right)$ | **9** |
| **29.3.50** | $\dfrac{\Gamma(k)}{(s+a)^k(s+b)^k}\quad (k>0)\quad 6$ | | $\sqrt{\pi}\left(\dfrac{t}{a-b}\right)^{k-\frac12} e^{-\frac12(a+b)t}I_{k-\frac12}\left(\dfrac{a-b}{2}\,t\right)$ | **10** |
| **29.3.51** | $\dfrac{1}{(s+a)^{\frac12}(s+b)^{\frac32}}$ | | $te^{-\frac12(a+b)t}\left[I_0\left(\dfrac{a-b}{2}\,t\right)+I_1\left(\dfrac{a-b}{2}\,t\right)\right]$ | **9** |
| **29.3.52** | $\dfrac{\sqrt{s+2a}-\sqrt{s}}{\sqrt{s+2a}+\sqrt{s}}$ | | $\dfrac{1}{t}\,e^{-at}I_1(at)$ | **9** |
| **29.3.53** | $\dfrac{(a-b)^k}{(\sqrt{s+a}+\sqrt{s+b})^{2k}}\quad (k>0)$ | | $\dfrac{k}{t}\,e^{-\frac12(a+b)t}I_k\left(\dfrac{a-b}{2}\,t\right)$ | **9** |
| **29.3.54** | $\dfrac{(\sqrt{s+a}+\sqrt{s})^{-2\nu}}{\sqrt{s}\sqrt{s+a}}\quad (\nu>-1)$ | | $\dfrac{1}{a^\nu}\,e^{-\frac12 at}I_\nu(\tfrac12 at)$ | **9** |
| **29.3.55** | $\dfrac{1}{\sqrt{s^2+a^2}}$ | | $J_0(at)$ | **9** |
| **29.3.56** | $\dfrac{(\sqrt{s^2+a^2}-s)^\nu}{\sqrt{s^2+a^2}}\quad (\nu>-1)$ | | $a^\nu J_\nu(at)$ | **9** |
| **29.3.57** | $\dfrac{1}{(s^2+a^2)^k}\quad (k>0)$ | | $\dfrac{\sqrt{\pi}}{\Gamma(k)}\left(\dfrac{t}{2a}\right)^{k-\frac12}J_{k-\frac12}(at)$ | **6, 10** |

| | $f(s)$ | | $F(t)$ | | |
|---|---|---|---|---|---|
| **29.3.58** | $(\sqrt{s^2+a^2}-s)^k$ | $(k>0)$ | $\dfrac{ka^k}{t}J_k(at)$ | | 9 |
| **29.3.59** | $\dfrac{(s-\sqrt{s^2-a^2})^\nu}{\sqrt{s^2-a^2}}$ | $(\nu>-1)$ | $a^\nu I_\nu(at)$ | | 9 |
| **29.3.60** | $\dfrac{1}{(s^2-a^2)^k}$ | $(k>0)$ | $\dfrac{\sqrt{\pi}}{\Gamma(k)}\left(\dfrac{t}{2a}\right)^{k-\frac{1}{2}}I_{k-\frac{1}{2}}(at)$ | | 6, 10 |
| **29.3.61** | $\dfrac{1}{s}e^{-ks}$ | | $u(t-k)$ | | |
| **29.3.62** | $\dfrac{1}{s^2}e^{-ks}$ | | $(t-k)u(t-k)$ | | |
| **29.3.63** | $\dfrac{1}{s^\mu}e^{-ks}$ | $(\mu>0)$ | $\dfrac{(t-k)^{\mu-1}}{\Gamma(\mu)}u(t-k)$ | | 6 |
| **29.3.64** | $\dfrac{1-e^{-ks}}{s}$ | | $u(t)-u(t-k)$ | | |
| **29.3.65** | $\dfrac{1}{s(1-e^{-ks})}=\dfrac{1+\coth\frac{1}{2}ks}{2s}$ | | $\displaystyle\sum_{n=0}^{\infty}u(t-nk)$ | | |
| **29.3.66** | $\dfrac{1}{s(e^{ks}-a)}$ | | $\displaystyle\sum_{n=1}^{\infty}a^{n-1}u(t-nk)$ | | |
| **29.3.67** | $\dfrac{1}{s}\tanh ks$ | | $u(t)+2\displaystyle\sum_{n=1}^{\infty}(-1)^n u(t-2nk)$ | | |
| **29.3.68** | $\dfrac{1}{s(1+e^{-ks})}$ | | $\displaystyle\sum_{n=0}^{\infty}(-1)^n u(t-nk)$ | | |
| **29.3.69** | $\dfrac{1}{s^2}\tanh ks$ | | $tu(t)+2\displaystyle\sum_{n=1}^{\infty}(-1)^n(t-2nk)u(t-2nk)$ | | |
| **29.3.70** | $\dfrac{1}{s\sinh ks}$ | | $2\displaystyle\sum_{n=0}^{\infty}u[t-(2n+1)k]$ | | |
| **29.3.71** | $\dfrac{1}{s\cosh ks}$ | | $2\displaystyle\sum_{n=0}^{\infty}(-1)^n u[t-(2n+1)k]$ | | |

| | $f(s)$ | $F(t)$ | |
|---|---|---|---|
| **29.3.72** | $\dfrac{1}{s}\coth ks$ | $u(t)+2\sum\limits_{n=1}^{\infty} u(t-2nk)$ | |
| **29.3.73** | $\dfrac{k}{s^2+k^2}\coth\dfrac{\pi s}{2k}$ | $|\sin kt|$ | |
| **29.3.74** | $\dfrac{1}{(s^2+1)(1-e^{-\pi s})}$ | $\sum\limits_{n=0}^{\infty}(-1)^n u(t-n\pi)\sin t$ | * |
| **29.3.75** | $\dfrac{1}{s}e^{-\frac{k}{s}}$ | $J_0(2\sqrt{kt})$ | 9 |
| **29.3.76** | $\dfrac{1}{\sqrt{s}}e^{-\frac{k}{s}}$ | $\dfrac{1}{\sqrt{\pi t}}\cos 2\sqrt{kt}$ | |
| **29.3.77** | $\dfrac{1}{\sqrt{s}}e^{\frac{k}{s}}$ | $\dfrac{1}{\sqrt{\pi t}}\cosh 2\sqrt{kt}$ | |
| **29.3.78** | $\dfrac{1}{s^{3/2}}e^{-\frac{k}{s}}$ | $\dfrac{1}{\sqrt{\pi k}}\sin 2\sqrt{kt}$ | |
| **29.3.79** | $\dfrac{1}{s^{3/2}}e^{\frac{k}{s}}$ | $\dfrac{1}{\sqrt{\pi k}}\sinh 2\sqrt{kt}$ | |
| **29.3.80** | $\dfrac{1}{s^\mu}e^{-\frac{k}{s}}\quad(\mu>0)$ | $\left(\dfrac{t}{k}\right)^{\frac{\mu-1}{2}}J_{\mu-1}(2\sqrt{kt})$ | 9 |
| **29.3.81** | $\dfrac{1}{s^\mu}e^{\frac{k}{s}}\quad(\mu>0)$ | $\left(\dfrac{t}{k}\right)^{\frac{\mu-1}{2}}I_{\mu-1}(2\sqrt{kt})$ | 9 |
| **29.3.82** | $e^{-k\sqrt{s}}\quad(k>0)$ | $\dfrac{k}{2\sqrt{\pi t^3}}\exp\left(-\dfrac{k^2}{4t}\right)$ | |
| **29.3.83** | $\dfrac{1}{s}e^{-k\sqrt{s}}\quad(k\ge0)$ | $\operatorname{erfc}\dfrac{k}{2\sqrt{t}}$ | 7 |
| **29.3.84** | $\dfrac{1}{\sqrt{s}}e^{-k\sqrt{s}}\quad(k\ge0)$ | $\dfrac{1}{\sqrt{\pi t}}\exp\left(-\dfrac{k^2}{4t}\right)$ | |
| **29.3.85** | $\dfrac{1}{s\sqrt{s}}e^{-k\sqrt{s}}\quad(k\ge0)$ | $2\sqrt{\dfrac{t}{\pi}}\exp\left(-\dfrac{k^2}{4t}\right)-k\operatorname{erfc}\dfrac{k}{2\sqrt{t}}=2\sqrt{t}\ \mathrm{i}\operatorname{erfc}\dfrac{k}{2\sqrt{t}}$ | 7 |
| **29.3.86** | $\dfrac{1}{s^{1+\frac12 n}}e^{-k\sqrt{s}}\quad(n=0,1,2,\ldots;\ k\ge0)$ | $(4t)^{\frac12 n}\ \mathrm{i}^n\operatorname{erfc}\dfrac{k}{2\sqrt{t}}$ | 7 |
| **29.3.87** | $s^{\frac{n-1}{2}}e^{-k\sqrt{s}}\quad(n=0,1,2,\ldots;\ k>0)$ | $\dfrac{\exp\left(-\dfrac{k^2}{4t}\right)}{2^n\sqrt{\pi t^{n+1}}}H_n\left(\dfrac{k}{2\sqrt{t}}\right)$ | 22 |
| **29.3.88** | $\dfrac{e^{-k\sqrt{s}}}{a+\sqrt{s}}\quad(k\ge0)$ | $\dfrac{1}{\sqrt{\pi t}}\exp\left(-\dfrac{k^2}{4t}\right)-ae^{ak}e^{a^2 t}\operatorname{erfc}\left(a\sqrt{t}+\dfrac{k}{2\sqrt{t}}\right)$ | 7 |

*See page II.

| | $f(s)$ | | $F(t)$ | |
|---|---|---|---|---|
| 29.3.89 | $\dfrac{ae^{-k\sqrt{s}}}{s(a+\sqrt{s})}$ | $(k\geq0)$ | $-e^{ak}e^{a^2t}\,\mathrm{erfc}\left(a\sqrt{t}+\dfrac{k}{2\sqrt{t}}\right)+\mathrm{erfc}\,\dfrac{k}{2\sqrt{t}}$ | 7 |
| 29.3.90 | $\dfrac{e^{-k\sqrt{s}}}{\sqrt{s}(a+\sqrt{s})}$ | $(k\geq0)$ | $e^{ak}e^{a^2t}\,\mathrm{erfc}\left(a\sqrt{t}+\dfrac{k}{2\sqrt{t}}\right)$ | 7 |
| 29.3.91 | $\dfrac{e^{-k\sqrt{s(s+a)}}}{\sqrt{s(s+a)}}$ | $(k\geq0)$ | $e^{-\frac{1}{2}at}I_0(\tfrac{1}{2}a\sqrt{t^2-k^2})u(t-k)$ | 9 |
| 29.3.92 | $\dfrac{e^{-k\sqrt{s^2+a^2}}}{\sqrt{s^2+a^2}}$ | $(k\geq0)$ | $J_0(a\sqrt{t^2-k^2})u(t-k)$ | 9 |
| 29.3.93 | $\dfrac{e^{-k\sqrt{s^2-a^2}}}{\sqrt{s^2-a^2}}$ | $(k\geq0)$ | $I_0(a\sqrt{t^2-k^2})u(t-k)$ | 9 |
| 29.3.94 | $\dfrac{e^{-k(\sqrt{s^2+a^2}-s)}}{\sqrt{s^2+a^2}}$ | $(k\geq0)$ | $J_0(a\sqrt{t^2+2kt})$ | 9 |
| 29.3.95 | $e^{-ks}-e^{-k\sqrt{s^2+a^2}}$ | $(k>0)$ | $\dfrac{ak}{\sqrt{t^2-k^2}}J_1(a\sqrt{t^2-k^2})u(t-k)$ | 9 |
| 29.3.96 | $e^{-k\sqrt{s^2-a^2}}-e^{-ks}$ | $(k>0)$ | $\dfrac{ak}{\sqrt{t^2-k^2}}I_1(a\sqrt{t^2-k^2})u(t-k)$ | 9 |
| 29.3.97 | $\dfrac{a^\nu e^{-k\sqrt{s^2+a^2}}}{\sqrt{s^2+a^2}(\sqrt{s^2+a^2}+s)^\nu}$ | $(\nu>-1,k\geq0)$ | $\left(\dfrac{t-k}{t+k}\right)^{\frac{1}{2}\nu}J_\nu(a\sqrt{t^2-k^2})u(t-k)$ | 9 |
| 29.3.98 | $\dfrac{1}{s}\ln s$ | | $-\gamma-\ln t\,(\gamma=.57721\,56649\ldots\,\text{Euler's constant})$ | |
| 29.3.99 | $\dfrac{1}{s^k}\ln s$ | $(k>0)$ | $\dfrac{t^{k-1}}{\Gamma(k)}[\psi(k)-\ln t]$ | 6 |
| 29.3.100 | $\dfrac{\ln s}{s-a}$ | $(a>0)$ | $e^{at}[\ln a+E_1(at)]$ | 5 |
| 29.3.101 | $\dfrac{\ln s}{s^2+1}$ | | $\cos t\,\mathrm{Si}\,(t)-\sin t\,\mathrm{Ci}\,(t)$ | 5 |
| 29.3.102 | $\dfrac{s\ln s}{s^2+1}$ | | $-\sin t\,\mathrm{Si}\,(t)-\cos t\,\mathrm{Ci}\,(t)$ | 5 |
| 29.3.103 | $\dfrac{1}{s}\ln(1+ks)$ | $(k>0)$ | $E_1\left(\dfrac{t}{k}\right)$ | 5 |
| 29.3.104 | $\ln\dfrac{s+a}{s+b}$ | | $\dfrac{1}{t}(e^{-bt}-e^{-at})$ | |
| 29.3.105 | $\dfrac{1}{s}\ln(1+k^2s^2)$ | $(k>0)$ | $-2\,\mathrm{Ci}\left(\dfrac{t}{k}\right)$ | 5 |
| 29.3.106 | $\dfrac{1}{s}\ln(s^2+a^2)$ | $(a>0)$ | $2\ln a-2\,\mathrm{Ci}\,(at)$ | 5 |

| | $f(s)$ | | $F(t)$ | |
|---|---|---|---|---|
| **29.3.107** | $\frac{1}{s^2}\ln(s^2+a^2)$ $(a>0)$ | | $\frac{2}{a}[at\ln a+\sin at-at\,\text{Ci}\,(at)]$ | 5 |
| **29.3.108** | $\ln\frac{s^2+a^2}{s^2}$ | | $\frac{2}{t}(1-\cos at)$ | |
| **29.3.109** | $\ln\frac{s^2-a^2}{s^2}$ | | $\frac{2}{t}(1-\cosh at)$ | |
| **29.3.110** | $\arctan\frac{k}{s}$ | | $\frac{1}{t}\sin kt$ | |
| **29.3.111** | $\frac{1}{s}\arctan\frac{k}{s}$ | | $\text{Si}\,(kt)$ | 5 |
| **29.3.112** | $e^{k^2s^2}\text{erfc}\,ks$ $(k>0)$ | 7 | $\frac{1}{k\sqrt{\pi}}\exp\left(-\frac{t^2}{4k^2}\right)$ | |
| **29.3.113** | $\frac{1}{s}e^{k^2s^2}\text{erfc}\,ks$ $(k>0)$ | 7 | $\text{erf}\,\frac{t}{2k}$ | 7 |
| **29.3.114** | $e^{ks}\text{erfc}\,\sqrt{ks}$ $(k>0)$ | 7 | $\frac{\sqrt{k}}{\pi\sqrt{t}(t+k)}$ | |
| **29.3.115** | $\frac{1}{\sqrt{s}}\text{erfc}\,\sqrt{ks}$ $(k\ge0)$ | 7 | $\frac{1}{\sqrt{\pi t}}u(t-k)$ | |
| **29.3.116** | $\frac{1}{\sqrt{s}}e^{ks}\text{erfc}\,\sqrt{ks}$ $(k\ge0)$ | 7 | $\frac{1}{\sqrt{\pi(t+k)}}$ | |
| **29.3.117** | $\text{erf}\,\frac{k}{\sqrt{s}}$ | 7 | $\frac{1}{\pi t}\sin 2k\sqrt{t}$ | |
| **29.3.118** | $\frac{1}{\sqrt{s}}e^{\frac{k^2}{s}}\text{erfc}\,\frac{k}{\sqrt{s}}$ | 7 | $\frac{1}{\sqrt{\pi t}}e^{-2k\sqrt{t}}$ | |
| **29.3.119** | $K_0(ks)$ $(k>0)$ | 9 | $\frac{1}{\sqrt{t^2-k^2}}u(t-k)$ | |
| **29.3.120** | $K_0(k\sqrt{s})$ $(k>0)$ | 9 | $\frac{1}{2t}\exp\left(-\frac{k^2}{4t}\right)$ | |
| **29.3.121** | $\frac{1}{s}e^{ks}K_1(ks)$ $(k>0)$ | 9 | $\frac{1}{k}\sqrt{t(t+2k)}$ | |
| **29.3.122** | $\frac{1}{\sqrt{s}}K_1(k\sqrt{s})$ $(k>0)$ | 9 | $\frac{1}{k}\exp\left(-\frac{k^2}{4t}\right)$ | |
| **29.3.123** | $\frac{1}{\sqrt{s}}e^{\frac{k}{s}}K_0\left(\frac{k}{s}\right)$ $(k>0)$ | 9 | $\frac{2}{\sqrt{\pi t}}K_0(2\sqrt{2kt})$ | 9 |
| **29.3.124** | $\pi e^{-ks}I_0(ks)$ $(k>0)$ | 9 | $\frac{1}{\sqrt{t(2k-t)}}[u(t)-u(t-2k)]$ | |
| **29.3.125** | $e^{-ks}I_1(ks)$ $(k>0)$ | 9 | $\frac{k-t}{\pi k\sqrt{t(2k-t)}}[u(t)-u(t-2k)]$ | |

| | $f(s)$ | | | $F(t)$ |
|---|---|---|---|---|
| 29.3.126 | $e^{as}E_1(as)$ $\quad(a>0)$ | | 5 | $\dfrac{1}{t+a}$ |
| 29.3.127 | $\dfrac{1}{a}-se^{as}E_1(as)$ $\quad(a>0)$ | | 5 | $\dfrac{1}{(t+a)^2}$ |
| 29.3.128 | $a^{1-n}e^{as}E_n(as)$ $\quad(a>0; n=0,1,2,\ldots)$ | | 5 | $\dfrac{1}{(t+a)^n}$ |
| 29.3.129 | $\left[\dfrac{\pi}{2}-\mathrm{Si}(s)\right]\cos s+\mathrm{Ci}(s)\sin s$ | | 5 | $\dfrac{1}{t^2+1}$ |

# References

**Texts**

[29.1] H. S. Carslaw and J. C. Jaeger, Operational methods in applied mathematics, 2d ed. (Oxford Univ. Press, London, England, 1948).

[29.2] R. V. Churchill, Operational mathematics, 2d ed. (McGraw-Hill Book Co., Inc., New York, N.Y., Toronto, Canada, London, England, 1958).

[29.3] G. Doetsch, Handbuch der Laplace-Transformation, vols. I–III (Birkhäuser, Basel, Switzerland, 1950; Basel, Switzerland, Stuttgart, Germany, 1955, 1956).

[29.4] G. Doetsch, Einführung in Theorie und Anwendung der Laplace-Transformation (Birkhäuser, Basel, Switzerland, Stuttgart, Germany, 1958).

[29.5] P. M. Morse and H. Feshbach, Methods of theoretical physics, vols. I, II (McGraw-Hill Book Co., Inc., New York, N.Y., Toronto, Canada, London, England, 1953).

[29.6] B. van der Pol and H. Bremmer, Operational calculus, 2d. ed. (Cambridge Univ. Press, Cambridge, England, 1955).

[29.7] D. V. Widder, The Laplace transform (Princeton Univ. Press, Princeton, N.J., 1941).

**Tables**

[29.8] G. Doetsch, Guide to the applications of Laplace transforms (D. Van Nostrand, London, England; Toronto, Canada; New York, N.Y.; Princeton, N.J., 1961).

[29.9] A. Erdélyi et al., Tables of integral transforms, vols. I, II (McGraw-Hill Book Co., Inc., New York, N.Y., Toronto, Canada, London, England, 1954).

[29.10] W. Magnus and F. Oberhettinger, Formulas and theorems for the special functions of mathematical physics (Chelsea Publishing Co., New York, N.Y., 1949).

[29.11] D. Voelker and G. Doetsch, Die zweidimensionale Laplace-Transformation (Birkhäuser, Basel, Switzerland, 1950).

# References

This is a subjective and eclectic list of references and applications in continuous-time finance that may be used to supplement and advance your study; it does not pretend to be complete. The references are organized by subject areas.

## Capital Market Equilibrium in Continuous Time Models

Breeden, Douglas, 1979, An intertemporal asset pricing model with stochastic consumption and investment opportunities, *Journal of Financial Economics* 7, 265-96.

Constantinides, George, 1989 Theory of valuation: An overview, in *Frontiers of Modern Financial Theory*, Sudipto Bhattacharya and George Constantinides, eds., Rowman and Littlefield.

Cox, J., J, Ingersoll, and S. Ross, 1985a, An intertemporal general equilibrium model of asset prices, *Econometrica* 53, 363-84.

Merton, R. C., 1986, Capital market theory and the pricing of financial securities, Working Paper #1818-86, Massachusetts Institute of Technology.

Merton, R. C., 1973, An intertemporal capital asset pricing model, *Econometrica* 41, 867-80.

## Cash Flow Valuation

Brennan, Michael J., 1973, An approach to the valuation of uncertain income streams, *Journal of Finance* 28, 661-74.

Constantinides, George, 1978, Market risk adjustment and project valuation, *Journal of Finance* 33, 603-16.

Dothan, Uri and Joseph Williams, 1980, Term-risk structures and the valuation of projects, *Journal of Financial and Quantitative Analysis* 15, 875-905.

Shimko, David C., 1989, The equilibrium valuation of risky discrete cash flows in continuous time, *Journal of Finance* 44, 1373-83.

## Option Pricing

Black, Fischer and Myron Scholes, 1973, The pricing of options and corporate liabilities", *Journal of Political Economy* 81, 637-59.

Geske, Robert, 1979, The valuation of compound options, *Journal of Financial Economics* 7, 63-82.

Geske, Robert and Herbert Johnson, 1984, The american put option valued analytically", *Journal of Finance* 39, 1511-24.

Geske, Robert and Kuldeep Shastri, 1985, Valuation by approximation: a comparison of alternative option valuation techniques, *Journal of Financial and Quantitative Analysis* 20, 45-72.

Longstaff, Francis A., 1990, The valuation of options on yields, *Journal of Financial Economics* 26, 97-121.

McDonald, Robert and Daniel Siegel, 1984, Option pricing when the underlying asset earns a below-equilibrium rate of return: A note, *Journal of Finance* 39, 261-65.

Merton, R. C., 1973, Theory of rational option pricing, *Bell Journal of Economics and Management Science* 4, 141-83.

Merton, R.C., 1976, Option pricing when underlying stock returns are discontinuous, *Journal of Financial Economics* 3, 125-44.

Roll, Richard, 1977, An analytic valuation formula for unprotected american call options on stocks with known dividends", *Journal of Financial Economics* 5, 251-58.

Smith, Clifford, 1976, Option pricing: A review, *Journal of Financial Economics* 3, 3-51.

Stulz, Rene M., 1982, Options on the minimum or the maximum of two risky assets: Analysis and applications, *Journal of Financial and Quantitative Analysis* 20, 391-406.

Wiggins, James B., 1987, Option values under stochastic volatility: theory and empirical evidence, *Journal of Financial Economics* 19, 351-72.

## The Term Structure of Interest Rates

Ahn, Chang Mo and Howard Thompson, 1988, Jump-diffusion processes and the term structure of interest rates, *Journal of Finance* 43, 155-74.

Brennan, Michael and Eduardo Schwartz, 1979, A continuous-time approach to the pricing of bonds, *Journal of Banking and Finance* 3, 133-55.

Cox, Ingersoll, and Ross, 1985b, A theory of the term structure of interest rates, *Econometrica* 53, 385-407.

Longstaff, Francis A., 1989, A nonlinear general equilibrium model of the term structure of interest rates, *Journal of Financial Economics* 23, 195-224.

Vasicek, O. A., 1977, An equilibrium characterization of the term structure, *Journal of Financial Economics* 5, 177-88.

## Mortgages and Mortgage–Backed Securities

Brennan, Michael and Eduardo Schwartz, 1985, Determinants of GNMA mortgage prices, *AREUEA Journal* 13, 209-28.

Dunn, Kenneth and J. J. McConnell, 1981, A comparison of alternative models for pricing gnma mortgage-backed securities", *Journal of Finance* 36, 471-83.

## Insurance Valuation

Cummins, David C., 1988, Risk-based premiums for insurance guaranty funds, *Journal of Finance* 43, 823-40.

Doherty, Neil A. and James R. Garven, 1986, Price regulation in property-liability insurance: A contingent-claims approach, *Journal of Finance* 41, 1031-50.

Shimko, David C., 1991, The valuation of multiple-claim insurance contracts, USC Working Paper.

## Other Contingent Claims

Brennan, M. and E. Schwartz, 1977, Savings bonds, retractable bonds and callable bonds, *Journal of Financial Economics* 5, 67-88.

Ingersoll, Jonathan E., Jr., 1977, A contingent claims valuation of convertible securities, *Journal of Financial Economics* 4, 289-322.

Smith, Clifford W., Jr., 1979, Applications of option pricing analysis, in James L. Bicksler, Ed., *Handbook of Financial Economics*, North Holland.

## Decision-Making

Brennan, Michael and Eduardo Schwartz, 1985, Evaluating natural resource investments, *Journal of Business* 58, 135–57.

McDonald, Robert, and Daniel Siegel, 1986, The value of waiting to invest, *Quarterly Journal of Economics* 101, 707–27.